A John Catt Publication

HIGH SCHOOL HACKS

HABITS OF MIND: SUCCESS IN THE IB AND BEYOND

BRIANNA SMRKE

First Published 2016

by John Catt Educational Ltd,
12 Deben Mill Business Centre, Old Maltings Approach,
Melton, Woodbridge IP12 1BL

Tel: +44 (0) 1394 389850 Fax: +44 (0) 1394 386893
Email: enquiries@johncatt.com
Website: www.johncatt.com

ISBN: 978 1 909717 75 6

Set and designed by Theoria Design Ltd

TABLE OF CONTENTS

ABOUT BRIANNA SMRKE

Brianna Smrke achieved a perfect 45 point score for her IB diploma at Michael Power St. Joseph HS in Toronto, Canada, a feat achieved by approximately one percent of IB students internationally.

This remarkable accomplishment was soon overshadowed by her exceptional university career, nearly completely funded by scholarships, where she was given the highest honor possible for an undergraduate at her institution, McMaster University.

While her engaging in her diverse studies (complex systems, social innovation, math, comics), travels (San Francisco, Bhopal, Cape Breton *etc*) and projects (cardboard carpentry, student refugee programs), she began to realize that the habits of mind she cultivated in IB were the engine of her success.

FOREWORD

I first heard of Brianna Smrke in the spring of 2014. Along with an exceptional group of colleagues, I am responsible for designing and delivering an annual conference. We bring educators together from all over the world, united by our common commitment to support the best education possible for students through the use of International Baccalaureate (IB) programmes.

Since 2007, we have asked IB graduates to attend the conference and introduce the major speakers, while reflecting upon the impact of the IB on their lives. Because of the success of this feature, there was nothing unusual about the call I received from Adrienne Murphy, who coordinated the IB Diploma Programme at Michael Power/St. Joseph High School in Toronto, from which Brianna graduated in 2010.

We knew this was going to be a big conference – it ultimately became the biggest event in the history of the International Baccalaureate Organization, with over 1700 attendees. Out of respect for Adrienne, I followed up with Brianna to see if she would be a good fit to introduce a speaker at the 2014 IB Conference of the Americas in Washington, DC.

That was when I began to learn more about this exceptional young scholar. First, I found out that she earned a "perfect" score of 45 on her IB Diploma. IB Diploma candidates take six international examinations that are scored on a scale of 1-7. Brianna received the top score of 7 on all six exams. Candidates also are scored on a matrix that provides up to 3 points for how they perform on the core elements of the program – a 4,000 research paper, a critical thinking class, and extracurricular activities with a focus on community service. Brianna received the maximum of three points, bringing her total score to 45. Less than one half of one percent of IB students worldwide achieve this ultimate standard of excellence.

I was duly impressed, but the point of bringing graduates to the conference was not merely to assemble those who received the highest scores, but rather those who were most profoundly impacted by the IB and have an important story to tell.

As Brianna's tale unfolded, it became clear to all of us that we were working with an exceptional individual, and that she represented both the opportunities and the challenges of the quest for a high score on the IB Diploma.

When she spoke to the conference attendees, she spent very little time talking about her perfect score, and much more time talking about how the IB helped prepare her to make the most of her life after secondary school. What a life it has been and what a life it is becoming!

While completing her undergraduate degree at McMaster University, Brianna co-founded and ran a student innovation space, the McMaster Social Innovation Lab, which involved an internship in Bhopal with AOSIS Social Innovations Laboratory, an organization dedicated to social entrepreneurship. She was part of the founding cohort of Studio Y, an eight-month immersive fellowship for young people who want to change systems - healthcare, education, and government. She wrote a graphic novel about systems thinking for her senior thesis, the first time that had happened in her program.

Brianna was selected as a 2013 3M National Student Fellow for her demonstrated leadership in the field of higher education. With the nine other fellows chosen from across Canada, she ran a national campaign called the Cult of Busy. This campaign questioned the frenetic pace of student and faculty life at many universities and colleges. She was part of the Founding Class of Minerva Schools @ KGI, an innovative university program that sends students around the world while they complete their degrees, and grounds all of its teaching practices in the science of learning. She provided feedback that helped shape the university's academic programs and student supports. At the moment, she is in the midst of a two-year internship program with the Ontario Public Service (OPS) Green Office, which works to reduce the government's environmental footprint and empower public servants to make greener choices every day.

I could go on, but I get tired just thinking of it. Brianna's life is undoubtedly complicated, but her message is simple – seek out opportunities and make the most of those opportunities to grow as a person and to change the world for the better. She used an analogy that stuck with all of us – instead of taking the escalator, take the stairs. It will be harder but you will see and do much more.

So it is with the IB Diploma Programme. The more you put into it, the more you will get out of it. Work hard to get a high score. Indeed, strive for perfection.

But remember, the lessons of the IB are not judged by your score on the IB Diploma. High scores are great, but high standards are better. Being admitted into a prestigious university is excellent, but the measure of university success is not where you get in, but how much you get out of it. Getting a great job is satisfying, but what will make you a success is whether you make things better for those close to you and those far away.

When I speak at IB graduation ceremonies, I offer only three pieces of advice. First, use the foundation that IB has provided to become fluent in at least one language other than your own. Second, stay deeply involved in community service. Third, deliberately seek out people who are different than you.

To these three, I now formally add a fourth:

Take the stairs.

Paul Campbell, Head of Outreach and Development
International Baccalaureate Americas

1 February 2016

INTRO

MOUSE TAILS AND MEDALS: AN INTRODUCTION

Toronto, Canada - July 6, 2010

I dropped my latest set of mouse tails into acid and sat back at the computer. On a whim, I opened my email and saw a new message from my IB Coordinator.

45...45...45...45...45...
What a lovely number that I enjoy writing.
Congratulations. How does it feel to achieve in the top 0.5% of all the IB students in the world?! Wow!
All the best
Mr S

If you can believe it, I was not that excited. In fact, I did not feel much at all. I turned back to the mouse tails, pipetting different solutions into the small tubes. Finally, I held them up to the light and marvelled at the tiny white threads of DNA.

The next day, videographers and photographers invaded the University of Toronto lab I worked in. I had to swirl beakers and look especially serious. It was a slow news day, so the following morning my face was plastered on major newspapers all over the city. I started my watch and waited for my 15 minutes of fame to end. Was it nice to be celebrated? Yes, definitely. But I also had a lurking sense that all of this fanfare was out of place. The game I was playing was just beginning.

Hamilton, Canada - November 22, 2013

I stared at the tiny metal disc in my hand. It faintly reminded me of Bertrand Russell's Nobel Prize. A few months earlier I had donned a pair of white gloves in my university's archives and gently touched the face of Alfred Nobel embossed on the surprisingly heavy medal. Now, I was touching my own name, which had been engraved into the smooth surface. It was the first award that meant anything to me. The Chancellor's Gold Medal is awarded to the one student in her graduating class who ranks highest in scholarship, leadership and influence. It meant that out of thousands of students in tens of disciplines, I had been judged worthy.

McMaster's President, Patrick Deane, began his commencement speech by speaking of Nobel Prizes. "They are an ultimate award," he said, "given after a lifetime of work, given after their holders have proved themselves brilliant and significant". "The degrees you now hold are placeholders. They have no value. They are waiting for you to prove yourselves. Your time begins now."

Sitting in the red corduroy seats, I realized that what I felt in that laboratory was the emptiness of a placeholder. I could not congratulate myself because I was not sure if I was worthy of congratulation. "Was it all a fluke?" I wondered. Holding the tiny medal on my palm, I decided that my success was most certainly not a fluke. The rules I lived by must be working. I was hit by an impulse to share my secrets with someone.

That someone is you. As a student in the IB program, you are me just a few years ago. I know the kind of pressures you are under. I remember the challenges you face. Yet, I also know the nearly limitless potential you have to excel in all aspects of your life. I want to give you the keys to unlock this potential.

I want to share the hard-fought learnings of my past 16 years of schooling, packaged into user-friendly chunks.

Let me assure you that this is not a textbook. You already have too many of those. It is a useful, hackable guide. Expect oddball examples, practical tips and valid evidence. Are you ready? Let's begin.

WHAT IF YOU FOUND
a way between
FIGHTING
&
CONFORMING?

TRANSFERABLE STRATEGIES

Most of the time, your life is not yours to control. You will need to take classes, do chores, and listen to others, even if you don't want to. Sometimes, you can walk away, and once in a while you can take control, but there is no way to win every battle. Fighting every single expectation or requirement that's placed on you is probably futile, and might not even be in your best interest.

But what if you found a third way between fighting and conforming? What if you were able to please others and yourself? People you think of as your enemies can become your allies. Activities you hated might become the ones that change your life's path. That's the point of this book. You can be free even while you are encased in a structure you didn't choose. You can make the rules work for you.

Before we move onto the 'how', let's make space for the 'why'. What made you pick up this book? Why do you want to make the rules work for you? Do you want to be seen as successful by others so that you will be given more respect and more resources to use for your own projects? Do you want to find a way to fold your deepest interests into everything you do? Do you want to form a strong net of relationships with interesting people because of your innocuous status as a student?

High school is a ticket to somewhere else. You can't do much these days without your diploma. And yet, with the right strategy, you can leave school with much more than a ticket. You can stuff these four years full of meaning and growth. I encourage you to think about what it is you want, what you dream about doing, and who you look up to. There is no reason why you can't start living these dreams now, even in little pieces. Make all of these future-focused things part of your life now.

You might want to be a writer. Why not get as much experience and feedback as you can? Why not submit the work you do for different classes to competitions or to be published in different places. Why not find ways to contact local writers when you need to do research or have a creative project?

Listen to your head and your heart. What is it that really interests you? What is it that you find yourself drawn to when you have a lot of free time? What do others tell you they see in you? Start with your own goals and dreams first. Then, we'll find a way to integrate them into the structure you step into at high school.

The important thing to remember is that you are the artist of your own life. There are many opportunities to personalize your experiences. Make your experience more than ordinary, and you will not regret it. Together we'll find out how. It is not as hard as you might think.

Before you decide what section to read next, write down one interest or goal that you want to use this book to pursue. The more specific, the better!

HOW IS THIS RELEVANT?

HOW DOES THIS APPLY TO IB?

If you came here expecting detailed instructions about how to score sevens on all of your IB exams, this book will disappoint you. Instead of being filled with academic tactics, this book is more of a guide to understanding and optimizing your whole self, from your brain to your relationships to your body. Why? Because while a focus solely on marks will probably work for you in high school, it does not set you up well for the stages to come. Focusing on improving yourself will help you achieve academic success, but it will also help you thrive in the challenging stages of your life that are yet to come.

Essentially, what this book offers you is a chance to overhaul the systems and processes you use to solve problems, make plans, and do things in your life. Essentially, I am teaching you to forage for your own berries and nuts. Rather than telling you exactly how to apply these tactics to your IB experience, I am giving you suggestions that need to be fleshed out based on your context. Nearly all of the information I write about in this book is meant to help you become an expert at changing your frame of mind and habits so that you are able to follow through on your intentions.

I am here to tell you that every change you make now will pay off handsomely in the years to come. You may feel that you have very little time now to make any changes in your life, but the perfect time to try something new will never materialize. Start small, and then let the benefits of your first success (in terms of added energy, or saved time) fuel the quest towards your next element.

How should you approach this book? It's not meant to be read cover-to-cover like a mystery novel. This book is more like a recipe book. You can take a look at all the dishes, decide which one you would like to try out, and then do it.

BEWARE THE BLOODY HAND:

OPTIMIZE YOUR *learning*

BEWARE THE BLEEDING HAND: THE CASE FOR KNOWING THE SCIENCE OF LEARNING

"I am sorry for the stains on the last three pages of this exam," I wrote. "I assure you that I do not have any kind of communicable blood disease." I felt sorry for the poor examiner who would have to contend with my work. In that sunny winter afternoon, sitting in my drafty classroom, I joined a small and strange club: People Who Have Bled on Their Exams by Accident. It might be a pretty exclusive group, but is nowhere near as neat as it sounds, trust me. At best, this anecdote reminds me of how under-optimized my study habits were in high school.

In grade school, I realized that if I wrote out something I needed to know for a test, I would remember it. It was as simple as that. It was a time-consuming but dependable way to ensure that I would never draw a blank.

In high school, too afraid to try something different for fear that it would backfire and cause me to bomb an assessment, I continued my writing habit. Three years in, I realized that my strategy was getting ridiculous for content-heavy courses like biology and history, but I persevered.

The fiercest test of my study routine was the IB history exam. I had to know over 40 single-spaced pages of events, analysis. Hours into my preparations, my hand began to blister. I slapped a band-aid onto my hand and kept going. It was this band-aid that unceremoniously fell off as soon as I began my history exam. The blister popped and started to bleed.

As I looked down at my paper, dotted with little red streaks, I thought, "There has to be a better way."

Back then, I hadn't discovered that there was a science to learning. I didn't know that countless hours of research have tested how people can best take in, understand, and remember information. I hadn't attended a school that drilled these strategies into me. Fortunately for you, dear reader, I bled so that you would not have to. In this section, we will cover ways to learn and study that, by the grace of science, are nearly guaranteed effective.

LEARN
LIKE YOU'D
SKETCH AN
ELEPHANT

MAKING ASSOCIATIONS

If you've ever seen great sketch artists start to draw something, you'll know that they follow a very particular format. First, they get the main gist of the shape they're drawing (let's say it's an elephant). They quickly draw the curve of the spine and a few blocky lines for the arms and legs. Next come the component shapes that make up the elephant. Circles, rectangles and triangles are joined together and plopped on top of the hasty framework. On top, they add the overall outline, and some shading. With a few final details, the picture comes to life.

You need to be a sketch artist when you are taking in information. If you start immediately shading and drawing the outline before you even know how big the elephant is, you're probably going to get stuck or make a mistake. You might make the ear way too big in comparison to the legs! Whenever you're reading or listening to something, try to develop a quick sketch or sense of the big picture. How long is this chapter? How many different concepts does it cover? How are they going to be presented? What kinds of patterns are being used. At this point, you just need to be skimming, reading headings and bolded words. The point is not to remember every word. The point is to remember how the words are strung together. If you see that a term gets discussed in detail later in the chapter, then you don't have to obsess over misunderstanding it at first glance. You might even want to leave more room in your notes to write in that additional information.

As you are reading and listening, it's also important to keep thinking about yourself. Yes, you. Think about your past experiences and knowledge. Is there any way to connect what you're learning now to another part of your life? Something you already know a lot about? If you can find and make these links, you make it more likely that this new information will be easier to remember. It also makes learning a bit more interesting. For example, if I am learning about dialysis,

I might think back to the heartbreaking documentary I watched about a young girl who was waiting for a kidney. The images and emotions from that experience might help me better understand and remember what it is I need to know for my biology test.

These kinds of examples are important, even if they aren't from your own life. Any time you can think of an example of something on your own, you are deeply processing the information. If you are having a hard time thinking of an example, try looking at ones that have been provided. What is similar about them? If you understand the rules behind an example, you also increase your understanding of the concept.

Sources

Conversation, Dr. Stephen Kosslyn, September 2014

IF IT'S FUNNY,
IT WILL STICK

THE ROLE OF HUMOUR IN LEARNING

If you see someone laughing while she is preparing for a math exam, you'd probably think she was either in the midst of a breakdown or well on her way to failing. In fact, injecting humour into your learning can help you remember concepts and reduce any anxiety that is keeping you from focusing.

Studies have shown that from elementary school to university, when teachers incorporate relevant humour (funny stories about class content) into their classrooms, students perform better, enjoy class more, and are more engaged. You may not be lucky enough to have a teacher who uses humour, but that should not stop you from being a wonderful, funny teacher for yourself.

"How do I find humour in my subjects?" you might be wondering. It's a great question. Answering it will help you with more than just your grades. Being able to amuse yourself and others with humour has been linked to a whole host of benefits. At a physical level, laughing releases endorphins and dopamine, reward chemicals in the brain. Laughing relaxes us, and can reduce feelings of pain and stress. At a cognitive level, laughing can increase our ability to be creative (probably because it lessens stress and anxiety), which enhances our problem-solving skills. Studies in the classroom have shown that humourous material is remembered better than neutral material.

Laughing makes you feel happier, but it also can make others happy. Sharing a joke with your friends or family can make you feel closer to them. People tend to admire the comedic skill of others. As you can probably now appreciate, you have every reason to strengthen your sense of humour. What better place to start than with your math notes? Using humour while studying is a low-risk way to start to challenge yourself to inject ordinary situations with humour.

Many people think that trying to analyze what makes funny things funny is like performing a vivisection on a frog (a vivisection is a dissection that is done on an animal while it is still alive). You might get answers, but you will kill the humour in the process. Still, there are some general theories of humour that you can use to guide your progress. We tend to laugh when there is a violation of expectations. If you were to watch a short film clip of a woman pushing a baby carriage along a street, and at the end of the clip the camera finally let you see inside the carriage, if there was a pig in there, you might start laughing, or at least smiling. It seems very silly to be pushing a pig in a carriage, doesn't it? This joke works better on a visual level than a verbal one, trust me!

One way to use humour in your studies is to create silly mental images of concepts you have to understand. Perhaps you need to understand the Krebs cycle (the process that oxygen-breathing organisms use to release energy from carbs, proteins, and fats). You know that a glucose molecule needs to be broken in half to make two pyruvate molecules, and that each of these pyruvate molecules is oxidized and loses another carbon from its backbone, before joining with an oxaloacetic acid molecule to make citric acid. Why can't you imagine this process as a series of surgeries. An unsuspecting glucose molecule wanted to get a nose job from a plastic surgeon but instead comes out as this Frankenstein citric acid molecule. Imagining the citric acid molecule screaming when it first sees its face in the mirror is pretty funny, and you have to admit that you will probably remember the process better than if you just tried to memorize the bland reaction steps.

Perhaps you think that this example is glaringly unfunny, or perhaps you are worried that the examples you produce won't be funny at all. It doesn't really matter. Unless you find what you've created to be hilarious, you probably won't be sharing these examples with anyone. Moreover, even if what you create isn't a laugh riot, you will have thought more deeply about the concepts you are studying, and, as we discuss in the Depth of Processing section, this will lead you to remember and understand them better than if you had spent the same amount of time simply reading your notes.

So, go forth, and be funny!

Sources

Stambor, Z. (2006). 'How laughing leads to learning'. *Monitor on Psychology*. American Psychological Association. www.apa.org/monitor/jun06/learning.aspx

N.a. (2009). 'Benefits of humor'. *This Emotional Life*. Public Broadcasting Station. www.pbs.org/thisemotionallife/topic/humor/benefits-humor

THE
DEPTH
OF YOUR
THINK ING
MATTERS

DEPTH OF PROCESSING

Let's say you're at a party and you meet two beautiful people. When one introduces himself as "Fred," you silently repeat his name to yourself in your head. When the second one introduces himself as "Harry," you connect the name in your mind to Prince Harry and Harry Potter, and imagine these three Harrys going for a romantic walk on the beach together. After a little bit of small talk, you move on to meet other people. At the end of the night, whose name do you think you are more likely to remember? You probably said Harry, but do you know why?

When you repeated the name Fred to yourself, you engaged in what cognitive scientists call shallow processing. Repeating a name will help you remember it a little, but because you have not made any other connections from the name to other information stored in your brain, it is less likely to stick than "Harry." Making the association between the Harry you just met and two other famous Harrys is an example of deeper processing. Creating the vivid mental image of them on a romantic walk furthers the depth of processing, making it easier to recall later. Interestingly, even if you just asked yourself whether you liked the sound of the name Harry or not, you probably would remember it better than the name you repeated. This occurs because evaluating something involves more processing than simply repeating it. Researchers have found that even when people are not told that they will be tested later, people who are instructed to engage in depth of processing (by classifying words, or generating images) do much better on memory tests than people who are given no specific instructions but told to prepare for the questions.

"If depth of processing really is a better way to learn, why aren't I doing it already?" you might be asking. Simply put, it is easier to learn something shallowly, and you probably have established beliefs and habits when it comes to studying. You might have a fixed mindset rather than a growth mindset (see our section on exactly that), believing that your skill in a subject is innate and can't really be enhanced. You might be used to studying by reading over the textbook or your notes. It can be scary to consider changing your habits, but there are countless studies that show that this change is the right decision.

You can incorporate depth of processing into your learning even when you are in the classroom. Instead of merely copying what the teacher has written for you, or filling out a handout, go deeper. Generate your own examples of concepts she is discussing. Maybe a character's dilemma in one of the novels you are reading reminds you of your sister. Write notes in the margins that comment on what you are learning. Think about the potential applications of what you are learning (could knowing about stem cells help you grow a new arm?), and ask questions. If you can think of a better way to define a term, use your own words. Drawing your own diagrams, maps and illustrations of concepts can also deepen your processing.

When you are preparing for tests, instead of re-reading your notes, give yourself practice tests. Force yourself to recall and write down important definitions, or solve practice questions (just make sure that you can quickly get feedback on your answers - have your notes ready or the solutions to the problems available). Make your studying active rather than passive. This way, you can quickly gauge where your gaps of knowledge are. If you failed to answer a few questionsz correctly, but breezed through most of the other sections of your practice test, you know where to focus your energy.

A word to the wise: when I said that these techniques were harder than the ones you probably use, I meant it. I would not recommend going cold turkey on shallow processing in favour of deep processing. Try the techniques in one class first, perhaps one where you feel relatively confident. Once you feel comfortable with these new practices, try to implement them in the class where you feel you are the weakest. I can understand the anxiety of trying out a new technique in a class where you struggle (what if it backfires?), but poor study habits are just amplifying the challenges you already face.

Sources

Chew, S. (2010). 'Improving classroom performance by challenging student misconceptions about learning.' *American Psychological Society Observer.* (23):2 www.psychologicalscience.org/index.php/publications/observer/2010/april-10/improving-classroom-performance-by-challenging-student-misconceptions-about-learning.html

MENTAL
IMAGERY
&
JPG
SPATIAL MEMORY

MENTAL IMAGERY + SPATIAL MEMORY

I have consulted and cited many different articles while writing this book, and each time I needed to cite one, I marvelled at the tiny capacity of my working memory. I usually failed to remember the article title, authors' names or publication date. I simply could not store all of this text in my mind. Finally, on a whim, I tried to visualize the information. I turned the authors' names into images. I imagined the first author, H. Roediger, as a hoe digging, and the second author, B. Finn, as a fish with fins. Then, I imagined them swimming across a daily calendar page emblazoned with the publication date. To my surprise, this clunky image stayed in my mind long enough to allow me to properly cite the source. Mental imagery is a powerful aid to memory. Competitors in the world memory championships use what they call a memory palace. They imagine a place they know well, usually their own homes, and then they place objects in each room that represent the information they need to remember. By imagining themselves walking through this memory palace, they can retrieve the objects in the correct order. When it comes to the objects themselves, it is important that they are as silly, oversized and remarkable as possible. They need to be memorable!

What makes the memory palace so effective is that it combines spatial and visual memory cues. Adding a spatial dimension to your memorizing of facts can help you learn them more reliably. Using visuals can also boost your memory, and, because coming up with these silly images is a creative task, it also makes studying more enjoyable. So, how can you use these kinds of techniques when you study?

If you are up for creating a memory palace, decide which place you want to imagine. It should be one that you know very well. It will help with your practicing if you are able to walk through the place, so the easiest location to choose might be your current place of residence. Memory palaces work best if you imagine a route that you walk through them, so decide what route you will be taking. Perhaps you can imagine that you are just getting home after school, so your route would involve you opening the door, hanging up your coat in the closet, getting a snack from the kitchen, walking to the living room, and then walking to your room. Once you have this order in mind (it might help you to walk the route a few times), you are ready to store images.

Turn whatever you have to remember into a series of images, whether it is the sequence of events that led to World War II or the components of the digestive system. Some topics will be easier to visualize than others, but working hard to come up with a good visual association for the difficult cases will help your memory in the long run. If you are stuck, try to come up with a visual for a word that rhymes with the idea you need to store. Always remember to make the visuals as flashy, memorable and maybe even gross as you can. Your next step is to distribute these visual objects in your memory palace. If the first thing you need to remember is the esophagus, imagine a giant, fleshy esophagus hanging from the doorknob to your home. Continue this with the other items you have to remember.

If the memory palace isn't your idea of a good time, the spatial-visual coupling works with many other objects. You could imagine a human body, and have your visual objects arranged at different parts along the body. Having a pre-defined order in which you always 'look' at the body, from the head to the toes, for example, is a great way to make sure you don't forget anything you've stored.

Using visual and spatial imagery is a great way to bring more creativity and colour to your studying routine. It also helps your memory. What's not to love?

Sources

Richards, R. 'Making it stick: memorable strategies to enhance learning'. *LD Online: The Educators' Guide to Learning Disabilities and ADHD.* www.ldonline.org/article/5602/

Pausello, Luciano. (2015).'Develop perfect memory with the memory palace technique'. *LiteMind.* www.litemind.com/memory-palace/

N.a. (2015). 'Improve your grade: mnemonics'. *Cengage Learning.* www.college.cengage.com/collegesurvival/wong/essential_study/6e/assets/students/protected/wong_ch06_in-depthmnemonics.html

TESTING

IS YOUR

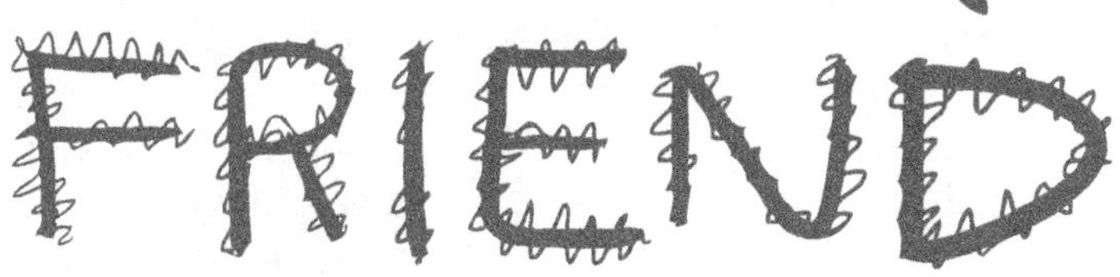

TESTING: YOUR MISUNDERSTOOD FRIEND

If you are like most students, you probably hate testing. Preparing for tests is time-consuming, stressful, and taking a test always carries with it a potential for failure. You might think that your life would be better without them. As happens with most blanket statements, you're not right, but you're also not totally wrong. Frequent testing can enhance learning, but the kind of tests that are administered really matters. Testing is not evil, it's just misunderstood.

Before we get into the difference between 'good' and 'bad' testing (at least when it comes to learning), let's understand what a 'good' test should allow you to do. Helping us in this quest is a distant cousin of the Johari window (the graphic you will encounter in our section about building self-knowledge). This four-square chart is called the Conscious Competence Learning Matrix, and emerged in the 1970s. According to the matrix, the goal of learning is for learners to move from unconscious incompetence to unconscious competence. Before they are exposed to a new skill or area of knowledge, learners do not know that they do not know it. Sometimes, even when people have been exposed to a new skill, without proper feedback they might not be aware of their incompetence (*eg* someone deciding that he is a great cook because he can fry an egg for breakfast while all of his room mates just eat cereal).

Testing can allow learners to compare their performance against an objective standard, and finally identify their incompetence. Correcting and perfecting their performance, through practice and review, can get them to the conscious competence state. You might be in this state if you can perform admirably at a task, but only if you concentrate very hard. You may be able to give a speech, but all the while you are reminding yourself to wiggle your toes to feel grounded, take deep breaths, and speak slowly. With more practice, this competence moves to the unconscious, and you no longer have to think about what you are doing. You have become unconsciously competent. Learning, at least the kind defined by this matrix, is a process of surfacing a behaviour from the unconscious mind, modifying it, and then sending it back down to the depths. While this model works more gracefully with skill acquisition, content learning can also be understood with these four steps.

Understanding this model also helps us understand what kind of testing is useful for learning. Testing must take place during learning, not after it. Testing should help students uncover areas of unconscious incompetence, and give them time to remedy these shortcomings. Accordingly, Dr. Henry Roediger III, a cognitive psychologist from Washington University, has found that summative assessments like the SAT do not help students learn. They merely assess what has been learned. While these tests are sometimes necessary to help sort and compare the performance of students and schools, the kind of test that helps enhance performance is called formative assessment. Formative assessments are short, low-stakes and informal activities that teachers use to monitor the progress of students. An example might be asking students to solve a mathematics problem similar to the one that was taught a few days ago. The results of these assessments are used to help students understand their weak areas and help teachers understand which areas they need to review.

"Sounds great," you say, "but my teacher doesn't do those." Luckily for you, you don't need him or her to be involved in order to get the benefits of formative assessments. You can do them yourself. Practice problems in your textbooks or online are ready-made formative assessments waiting for you to use them. Testing is not your enemy, it is a friend that can save you time by helping you focus your effort. Testing can make you conscious of your areas of incompetence so you can turn them to competence.

Sources

Lahey, J. (2014). 'Students should be tested more, not less'. *The Atlantic.* www.theatlantic.com/education/archive/2014/01/students-should-be-tested-more-not-less/283195/

Van Veekhout, V. (2010). 'Conscious competence learning matrix'. https://vincentvaneekhout.wordpress.com/2010/01/08conscious-competence-learning-matrix/

THE
WEB
IS YOUR
TEXTBOOK

LURK AND YE SHALL FIND

In Grade 11, it was a relatively common occurrence for my classmates to come up to me and ask: "Can you add me to your list? Please?" What kind of list, you ask? You might be imagining something sinister or adventurous. Perhaps it was list of people I would allow into my bunker in the event of a nuclear attack by North Korea. Perhaps it was a list of people whose names I would agree to have tattooed on my first-born child. The truth is a little less colourful. These students wanted to be added to my academic mailing list. Whenever I came across a resource that was helpful for studying, I sent it hurtling through cyberspace to my friends, frenemies, and acquaintances.

I found it a little strange that my friends hadn't already found these resources on their own. I mean, wasn't it standard practice to ask 'Auntie Google' (feel free to call her that now as well) whether there were premade quizzes or full syllabi for different classes? The more people I talked to, the more I realized that it definitely was not standard practice. For whatever reason, my fellow students had not thought of the internet as a place to accelerate their learning. It is time that this thinking changed.

What made me different from most of my friends is that I refused to put the fate of my learning in someone else's hands. If my teacher explained a concept poorly (or I just failed to understand it), or if my textbook was too general or had few practice questions, I did not give up. I simply looked elsewhere. I was resourceful. Resourcefulness is about taking control of your own learning. It is about embracing the democratization of information that has become normal in the internet age. Now, more than ever before, no one but you gets to decide the quality of your learning experience.

As International Baccalaureate students, we are privileged to be part of a global network of learners and teachers. With students in Singapore studying the same materials as those in Bogota, there are many opportunities to benefit from resource-sharing. All you have to do is type the right terms into a search engine and start panning for gold. The effort-reward ratio is so low that it is always worth checking.

I could recreate Brianna's academic mailing list and showcase a few websites that I think are especially helpful, but with how fast things can change on the internet (one of the biology websites I used to consult has now been turned into a clearinghouse for so-badly-written-they-might-be-spam blog posts), I think it might be better to teach you how to find and assess resources for yourself.

> Here are three questions you should ask yourself whenever you're trying to determine whether a resource is legitimate.
>
> 1. Who wrote this? *Was this website created by a class? A group of students? A group of teachers?*
>
> 2. Is the information accurate? *If you match up a few random samplings to your textbook or another trusted resource, do they match up?*
>
> 3. Is the information useful? *Does it explain concepts in a way that you find more intuitive? Are there practice problems? Is it easy to get feedback?*
>
> 4. BONUS: Would I share this with 30 of my peers? *Treat yourself as you would treat your friends. If it is not good enough for them, it certainly is not good enough for you!*

If you do come across a resource that is fantastic, be sure to express your gratitude. Know that what you are reading is probably the result of hours of underappreciated work. Marvel at the care these internet citizens took to share their knowledge, and then send them a little email, or comment on their About page. I mention this to you because I have a confession to make. I have internet sins for which I must atone (no, not THOSE kind of internet sins). I am a perennial lurker. To lurk means to read without commenting, liking or doing any kind of contributing. For years, I benefitted from quizzes and resources posted by others, but I never thanked them. In recent time, I have come to regret this behaviour. I realize now that a practice of gratitude can add as much to my own life as it adds to the experience of others.

That was a surprising amount of moralizing for a chapter about internet resources, but as Forrest Gump would say, this book is like a box of chocolates. You never quite know what you're going to get, but chances are it will be pretty sweet!

FIND SAFE
fail
GAME
OVER
ZONES

FINDING SAFE FAIL ZONES

Growing your knowledge and talents requires brushing up against the edges of your current capabilities. In other words, you have to take a few falls in order to find your blind spots. Failure is cringe-inducing because we often think of it in the context of high-risk, high-pressure situations. You might blank out while sitting to write an exam, or flub a basket in the fourth quarter of your semi-final game. Those failures are high profile, and they sting, but not all failures are like that. I actually grew to love the many mistakes I made while completing reams of math problems. I knew that if I found and corrected a mistake I had made while applying a concept or deciphering a word problem, then I was unlikely to make it again. Making an error made the concept stick strongly in my mind. In fact, it was the concepts I had applied correctly that I had to make sure to thoroughly review!

My experience aligns with a recent study of how errors help our learning. Research from the University of California at Los Angeles (UCLA), showed that students who were given a chance to make and correct a mistake tended to remember information better than students who were just given the correct information to study. As we know from our Depth of Processing section, trying to recall an answer engages our mind more deeply, and makes the information more likely to stick in our minds. Making and correcting a mistake also focuses our attention on the concept.

Even asking ourselves questions we are bound to get wrong can enhance our learning and memory. Research out of the University of California Irvine showed that when students had to answer questions about concepts they had never read about, they remembered the concept better once they learned it, compared to students who were just given extra time to study. When reading new material, you should put this principle to work for you. For example, when learning about the kidney, before you read a definition of a nephron, try to guess what it is. Then, check yourself with the real definition. You will likely be wrong, but that's fine, because you've just helped the right information stick into your mind!

It is clear, then, that mistakes can be awesome helpers when we are trying to learn. The kinds of mistakes that can help you are more likely to be small, low-risk ones that don't trigger feelings of shame. I like to call these mistakes 'safe-fails', because they don't put you or anyone else in danger. These fails are part of the learning process, and, especially if you hack your learning process by forcing yourself to fail, you aren't even expecting yourself to get any individual question right, so you probably won't feel ashamed if you do!

There are two ways to put these safe-fails to work for you. The first, as we've just talked about, is to question yourself before learning or reviewing. Your textbooks are set up to make this kind of safe-failing possible. Instead of reading over the chapter, skip to the review questions. Try to answer them, and then start reviewing. Correct your mistakes. To cement what you've just reviewed, try the questions again. If you want to see whether this approach is really working for you, try to compare your understanding of sections you studied with the pre-test method to sections you reviewed normally. My bet is that you will notice a difference!

The second way to make failure work for you is to make an error list. I loved doing this, especially when I was reviewing math. Once you have completed a set of problems, or even once you have been returned a marked test or assignment, take a look at your errors. Write down the correct way to do things. Perhaps you forgot that (a+b)^2 is not the same as a^2 + b^2. By writing the mistake and the correct way down, you are much less likely to make the same mistake again.

Once you incorporate these two techniques into your academic process, I am sure that you will come to love your little mistakes, just like I did. They really are gifts, because when they happen, you know that if you handle them correctly, you are much less likely to fail when it really counts.

Sources

Roediger, H., and Finn, B. (2009, October 20). "Getting it wrong: surprising tips on how to learn". *Scientific American*. www.scientificamerican.com/article/getting-it-wrong/

MINDFULNESS

MINDFULNESS STARDUST: MINDFULNESS

Mindfulness is a bit of a fad right now, and if you are aware of it, it may seem silly to you. Why ignore the past and future simply to focus on the present moment? Why mute your internal monologue of judgment? What even is there to experience if you limit yourself to what is around you, your body, and your mind? Let's find out right now.

You are made of atoms. These atoms have been cycling in and out of different forms of matter since the beginning of time. Some of them might have been part of a dinosaur. Most of them have been inside stars. Every single physical object around you has this hidden atomic history.

If you look around you, you will probably see manufactured objects. Think about where they were made, and by who. Think of all the metal springs inside your mattress. The metal needed to be mined from pits deep in the ground. Cotton for your sheets might have come from a plantation in India. Think of all the people who were involved in making everything around you, and all of the borders that were crossed so that the materials of your life could find their way to you.

Consider your breath. As you take air into your lungs, blood is rushing through capillaries, and oxygen is being exchanged for carbon dioxide. Think of the DNA inside of all of your cells, without which you would be nothing but an inert pile of minerals and organic chemicals. Consider all of the activity in your brain at the moment, the symphony of electrical impulses that lights up different functional areas like a series of lightning strikes.

Consider your emotions and thoughts. Marvel at them without judgment. Accept them all.

If you can feel the sun on your face, marvel at how far it has travelled to reach you. Think about the infinite universe that is expanding all around you. There is so much waiting to be experienced within the present moment. It is just a matter of being able to appreciate it. If you are not looking for it, you will not see it.

Mindfulness transmutes all of these thoughts into a rich, wordless awareness of one's being in the world and the universe. A team of researchers led by Dr. Scott Bishop of the University of Toronto have distilled a definition of mindfulness down to two parts. First, a person is being mindful when they are able to keep their attention in the present moment, and consider their immediate experiences. Considering the metal springs in one's bed qualifies if the bed is in view, as does recognizing angry emotions. The second component of mindfulness is the attitude a person has towards the objects of their attention. A mindful person does not judge anything they see as good or bad. Instead, they accept and experience their thoughts and emotions with curiosity and acceptance. Why is a lack of judgment important? Judgment takes us away from the present moment. It invokes perspectives and opinions that have been formed in the past, or absorbed from other sources.

After a three-month course on mindfulness, I began to understand its power. Practicing non-judgmental awareness gave me a deep sense of inner peace, and a renewed awareness of the richness of my experience. I grew these gifts within my mind, and was comforted by the knowledge that they could never be taken away from me. Mindfulness has given me an anchor to hold fast to when faced with the tumult of information and choices of my day-to-day life. It has allowed me to truly relax and recharge my mind and spirit.

My experience with mindfulness could be a throwaway anecdote, but there are mounting piles of evidence that the practice can greatly enhance mental and physical health. Research studies published in journals like *Psychological Science* have shown mindfulness can reduce stress, make it easier to go to sleep, increase verbal reasoning ability, increase compassion, and even protect against mental illness.

How can you introduce mindfulness into your life? The following sections will give you realistic suggestions and activities. Start now: you will thank yourself later.

Sources

Chan, A. (2013). 'Mindfulness Meditation Benefits: 20 Reasons Why It's Good For Your Mental And Physical Health'. *Huffington Post Healthy Living*. www.huffingtonpost.com/2013/04/08/mindfulness-meditation-benefits-health_n_3016045.html

Bergland, C. (2013). 'Mindfulness made simple'. *Psychology Today*. www.psychologytoday.com/blog/the-athletes-way/201303/mindfulness-made-simple

Greenberg, M. (2012). "Nine essential qualities of mindfulness." *Psychology Today*. www.psychologytoday.com/blog/the-mindful-self-express/201202/nine-essential-qualities-mindfulness

Bishop, S. R., Lau, M., Shapiro, S., Carlson, L., Anderson, N. D., Carmody, J., Segal, Z. V., Abbey, S., Speca, M., Velting, D. and Devins, G. (2004). 'Mindfulness: a proposed operational definition'. Clinical Psychology: Science and Practice, 11: 230–241. www.jimhopper.com/pdfs/bishop2004.pdf

STARTING
TO BE
MINDFUL
BUS STOP

STARTING TO BE MINDFUL

You may have read our first section on mindfulness and bought my argument that it is a highly valuable state of mind, but the practice might still be intimidating to you. You probably have visions of monks in orange robes sitting for hours staring at a wall, but incorporating mindfulness into your life doesn't require extreme measures. You might not even have to add more than ten minutes to your daily schedule. Simple tweaks to activities you already engage in can make your day more calm and rich. To prove it, let's venture through a day in your life, and identify opportunities to practice mindfulness.

A word before we start: all of these tweaks involve slowing the mental chatter in your head. You are probably used to having an internal voice running in the back of you head, providing silent commentary on your day. This voice transports you into the past (worrying about or rehashing what just happened) or the future (planning for what might happen). When I was first learning about mindfulness, Omer, a friend of mine, told me about his trick for clearing his mind. He imagined these thoughts as bubbles that he could flick out of his head with an imaginary set of fingers. He also reminded me never to get mad at myself if thoughts kept cropping up (mindfulness is all about being non-judgmental, remember), but to simply and calmly flick them away. With that said, let's begin.

Good morning! You've just regained consciousness after eight hours of sleep. Your current habit might be to immediately check your phone or laptop, but how about making a small change? Before you do anything, take ten large box breaths (four-count inhale, four-count hold, four-count exhale, four-count hold), and feel your lungs expand and compress. Then, stretch! Pay attention to your body. Notice how your muscles scream out as you pull them tight. This tweak probably won't add very much time to your routine, but I guarantee that the box breathing will make you feel calm, and that stretching will wake up your body.

What's next? I can't know for sure the order in which you get everything done, but I am pretty confident that your morning routine involves getting dressed, eating breakfast, brushing your teeth, washing your face, and finding your way to school. This entire routine is fertile ground for being mindful. Why not feel the texture of your clothes before you put them on, and appreciate their hues? Why not smell your cereal before you take your first bite? I am sure that you can think of many ways to enhance and enrich what you do every morning.

You might be raising a skeptical eyebrow right now. Being mindful often forces you to slow down, and sometimes, mornings are times when every minute is precious (especially when you have a bus to catch!). I would not recommend that you try to make every part of your morning routine mindful all at once, but I think that committing to enriching one part of your routine, whether it is brushing your teeth or tying your shoes, can go a long way. You can always add more later. The important thing is just to start!

But let's get back to your day. By now, you are probably waiting for the bus. Time spent waiting usually is a prime time to check your phone, or for worrying about what needs to be done when the waiting is over, but it can also be a great opportunity to focus on your breathing. When you are waiting somewhere by yourself, whether you are in line at the cafeteria, or in front of the TV ignoring commercials, try to bring yourself into a mindful state. Wiggling your toes is one way to raise your awareness of your body. Examining what is happening around you from a non-judgmental, curious perspective is another way to be present.

I'd encourage you to focus during your classes, but in the moments of transition between your courses, notice all the sights and sounds around you as people hurry off to the next classroom. If your day involves exercise, you're in luck. There is so much to notice when you work out, from the heat emanating from your skin to the pace of your breath. If you're wondering about food, we have a whole section on mindful eating so that you can satisfy your curiousity.

In short, a mindful tomorrow is in your reach. Adapt any one of these activities to your life, and you'll be well on your way.

Sources

Tartakovsky, M. (2012). 'Seven easy ways to be mindful every day'. *World of Psychology*. www.psychcentral.com/blog/archives/2012/06/09/7-easy-ways-to-be-mindful-every-day/

Mindful Eating

MINDFUL EATING

Toddler me was a messy eater. There are plenty of pictures of me with pasta sauce all over my face and bib. As soon as I was allowed to feed myself, I would spend almost as much time putting food on my face and body as I would putting it in my mouth. My mother, always my staunch defender, explained to my dad that I was 'experiencing' my food. To this day, I have a predisposition for 'experiencing' my food. I no longer smear it all over my face, but I pay extra attention to how it looks, smells, feels and tastes. I am a natural mindful eater.

Mindfulness might still seem intimidating to you, but in this section we will talk about an excellent opportunity for mindfulness that happens at least three times a day. This section also gives me an excuse to wax poetically about eating. I mean, have you ever stopped to think about the fact that we need to eat so reliably? Our bodies are actually using what we eat to power our brains, muscles, and organs. Eating is a reminder of how fragile we are. We need fuel. And yet, eating is also usually a demonstration of human ingenuity. If food was merely fuel, we would just be content to eat bland but healthful dishes. We might even have nutrients injected intravenously. Most of us don't. Meals are more than just fuel. They are chances to connect with other people, and to take real pleasure from flavourful food. Eating is a necessity and a luxury at the same time.

Of course, there are times when our eating habits tend towards the utilitarian. Usually this happens because of time or emotional pressures. Perhaps you're used to scarfing down breakfast while you are on the bus to school. Or, maybe you eat lunch without really thinking of it, because you are too busy checking your phone for updates. Think back to what you ate today. Think also about how you ate it. Is there room for enrichment? There probably is. Mindful eating is one way you can transform these situations so that they boost your physical and mental health. All you need is yourself.

Eating mindfully means focusing on the immediate experience of your food. What does it look like? What does it smell like? What is the texture of the soft bread in your hands? Does the slice of turkey taste salty or smoky? Is your chocolate milk more creamy than white milk? Looking inquisitively at your food will help you realize how much beauty there is even in a simple sandwich. Mindful eating is also about focusing on your own feelings. Are you hungry? Tired? Is your stomach growling? Can you feel the food filling your stomach? How do you know when you are full? Finally, mindful eating is about cultivating feelings of gratefulness for the food you are eating. Think about the person who made your sandwich, and the farmers that grew the tomatoes that made their way into your salad.

Mindful eating cannot happen when you are reading a book, watching TV, or walking to school. If another task is taking your full attention, eating turns into a mindless habit. Eating mindlessly can be dangerous because you learn to be less attentive to the state of your body. You probably have all had the experience of eating more potato chips than you wanted to, all because you had the bag with you while you were watching television. If you continue a pattern of mindless eating, you will start to want to eat more than you should. These tendencies can be undone, but it takes quite a bit of work, so it is better to avoid it altogether.

You might already be thinking about the barriers that prevent you from eating mindfully. First on your mind might be the presence of others. What if there are other people around you? You probably have no desire to be the weird kid who insists on sniffing their salad before they take a bite. One important thing to note about mindful eating is that it is not an all-or-nothing game. Eating a single meal or snack in a more mindful manner each day is fantastic. It makes sense to be strategic about which meal or snack you choose. Perhaps breakfast works better for you. Or, maybe you are confident that you can get your family on board with eating dinner mindfully. If you are eating mindfully in a group, conversation is still allowed! Most of it just has to be about the food itself. Try it and see if it works for you. Otherwise, eating snacks mindfully might be your best bet.

The second constraint to keep in mind is that mindful eating tends to take longer than normal eating. This might not be a problem for a snack, but if you are planning to eat your breakfast mindfully, and know that you have to catch a bus, you might want to start eating a little bit earlier, rather than having to abort the experiment part way through.

Mindful eating is a simple way to enrich your life. I encourage you to pretend that you were three-year-old me and go 'experience' your food.

Sources

Clancy, J. (2010). 'How to master the art of mindful eating'. *Zen Habits*. http://zenhabits.net/mindful-eating/

GRATITUDE

GRATITUDE AND MINDFULNESS

Gratitude and mindfulness are probably soul mates. One leads so easily to the other, and both have bonafide health benefits. Gratitude is an emotion of the present and past. Appreciating what we have, who loves us, where we are, and what we see can add so much richness into our lives. Yet, most of the time, we don't do it. We don't think about the fact that we are alive and healthy as opposed to ill or dead, we don't think about the people that surround us and care for us, because we assume they will always be there. Because we can count on them continuing to exist for us, these things all become unremarkable.

By denying ourselves the chance to be grateful, we are preventing ourselves from enjoying the benefits of the practice. Research studies that compare people who practice gratitude to people who don't have found that the first group tends to be physically healthier, better slept, more mentally resilient, happier, more social, and less lonely. However, most of these studies can't prove causation. They just show that people who rank higher on gratitude tend to rank higher on other traits. Smart readers that you are, you are probably protesting, "Well, what if they are just more grateful because they have more to be thankful for? What if they do have great health, a strong financial status, and lots of love around them? The gratitude might just be a symptom of a better life". You're right. Still, there is a strand of research that does show how gratitude can cause these benefits. Dr. Robert Emmons recruits participants to his studies that do not currently practice gratitude. He tests all of them for certain traits, and then randomly chooses a subgroup that he instructs to start writing in a gratitude journal (exactly what it sounds like – a place to write about the things they are thankful for). After a few weeks, everyone is given the same tests and the results are compared. People who start gratitude practices experience the same types of benefits as were found in the other studies. Gratitude has a power all of its own.

Emmons has a few theories as to why gratitude is so good for us. He suggests that feeling grateful for something actually increases our enjoyment of it in the future, because we are more focused and aware of it. Feeling grateful for a meal and then eating it will probably give us a better experience than eating the meal distractedly in front of a television. Gratitude brings us more into the present and enriches our experience of it, feeding into a spiral of positive emotion. Gratitude also strengthens our relationships with others. Feeling appreciated by someone else makes us feel better, and also increases the chance that we will want to befriend that person, or help him or her in the future. Fittingly, it increases the likelihood that we will have more things to be grateful for.

The fact that gratitude is so good for us does not mean that it is an easy practice to keep up. Even Emmons admits that he struggles with maintaining a consistent practice, despite the fact that he has been studying the benefits of thankfulness for decades! I find that a mindfulness practice naturally leads to thankfulness, so if you are already trying to become more mindful, great for you! Another, more physical approach that you can take, one that will help you capitalize on the relational benefits of gratitude, is writing 'Thank you' cards. Buying yourself a pack of cards, keeping them on your desk, and creating a habit where you write and send (or even hand-deliver) one a week is a wonderful way to begin to be more grateful. Your letters could be to people you know, but they also might be to inanimate objects like the sun. It would be very dangerous to try to give a card to the sun, so keep the ones that have no human recipients in the bottom of your card set, and look over them when you are in need of reminders. Very specific thank-yous are more effective for you and others than vague ones. If you appreciate your mother, tell her about a few instances where you really felt her love (maybe it was the scarf she knit for you, or the time she coached your hockey team). As you are writing them, try to really feel the positive emotions of love and thankfulness that are coming up. Think deeply about the situation and all of the details of how it made you feel. These strategies have all been proven to boost the effects of a gratitude practice, and make you more likely to continue it.

If you follow them, you might get hooked on gratitude. It's an addiction of which I thoroughly approve!

Sources

Carter, C. (2014). 'How to practice radical gratitude'. *Greater Good: The Science of a Meaningful Life*. www.greatergood.berkeley.edu/article/item/how_to_practice_radical_gratitude

Emmons, R. (2010). 'Why gratitude is good'. *Greater Good: The Science of a Meaningful Life*. www.greatergood.berkeley.edu/article/item/why_gratitude_is_good/

INTRUSIONS &
the
ORGANIZED
MIND

THE UPSIDE OF ORGANIZATION

To be present, you usually have to be organized. Doesn't that sound like a contradiction? Organization implies planning for the future, and considering events from the past. It ignores the present completely. And yet, when we are organized, we can better stay in the present. Why? Our explanation starts in the 1920s, with a Lithuanian psychologist sitting in a diner. She notices that the waiters have no trouble remembering lengthy orders before they are filled, but once the food has been delivered, the information seemed to vanish from their minds. The psychologist, named Bluma Ziegarnik, decided to test this phenomenon in her lab. She found that when people were given problem solving tasks and then interrupted, they remembered much more detail than people who were allowed to complete the tasks. This memory phenomenon soon became known as the Ziegarnik Effect.

Almost 100 years later, psychologists are still doing research along the same lines. They have come up with some surprising insights. Baumeister and Maiscampo discovered that if people are given a task but not allowed to finish it, they perform much more poorly on a subsequent task than others who were allowed to finish the first. The first group seems to be preoccupied with thoughts of the incomplete task. However, the psychologists found that if the participants were allowed to make a specific plan for how to complete the task, the negative effects vanished. A different study at Florida State University looked at the effect of creating plans for unfinished tasks on the ability of students to focus while reading an article, and found similar results. Creating a plan that you intend to execute later seems to be just as good as completing a task when it comes to stopping intrusive thoughts about what remains undone. Planning gives us a sense of closure. That is why having an organized life allows you to be more present. Without it, thoughts of unfinished business would constantly intrude into your mind while you are trying to focus on what is important to you.

I stumbled across this effect by accident, and for years I didn't really understand how to harness it for myself. I remember being so relieved when I finished school each year and headed into summer. I knew that I was going to be more present in my own life. I knew that at my jobs, unlike at school, I would not have work hanging over my head. I did not have to concern myself with unfinished tasks. I hated the feeling of having long and complicated tasks (writing my extended essay, or applying to universities) hanging over my head. These feelings continued, and even worsened, as I journeyed through my undergraduate degree. I remember loving classes that had weekly assignments much more than ones where large term papers would loom in the background of my mind. I still did not realize that I was in control of my experience! It wasn't until I was faced with the challenge of writing my book that I realized I could set up a healthy and productive work plan for myself.

As we'll discuss in the section called One Bite at a Time, I finally found a way to remove that heavy feeling of unfinished business. Breaking large tasks into small chunks that could be finished in one sitting gave me the momentum to keep going forward (as each chunk was manageable), but also allowed me to feel great at each step. Writing this book could have been a terrible experience for me; it was the largest project I had ever tackled. But, by developing a plan that allowed me to be finished each day once I hit a certain word count, I was able to feel as though I had completed a task each day, instead of feeling the weight of all the words I had yet to write. I managed to avoid the Ziegarnik Effect by shrinking the scale of my task so that I could always finish it in a day.

Getting things done doesn't need to make you miserable. A good, specific plan can help you waltz through your life. You don't need to be trapped under the weight of unfinished tasks. Break them into pieces and focus on what you can finish in the moment. Organization and planning might sound boring, but it is a surefire way to free up mental space for an interesting life.

Sources

Stoffard, T. (2013). 'The Psychology of the To-Do List'. *BBC Brain*. www.bbc.com/future/story/20130129-the-psychology-of-the-to-do-list

Dean, J. (2011). 'The ziegarnik effect'. *PsyBlog*. www.spring.org.uk/2011/02/the-zeigarnik-effect.php

Kageyama, N. (2015). 'How to get those distracting thoughts out of your mind when you're trying to practice'. *Bulletproof Musician*. www.bulletproofmusician.com/how-to-get-those-distracting-thoughts-out-of-your-head-when-youre-trying-to-practice/

WELLNESS

DEVICE-FREE DOWNTIME

HELPS YOUR BRAIN!

TECHNOLOGY AND OUR BRAINS I: THE IMPORTANCE OF DOWNTIME

I've struggled with how to approach this section on building focus because it's very clear that the odds are stacked against us. Screens have invaded our lives. We watch and interact with them for hours every day. Were we ever to step away from them, these devices call us back to them with buzzes, beeps and bells, rewiring our brains to be on the constant lookout for new information. The verdict is in. You, I and scientists know that personal technology is eroding our ability to focus on, learn, and remember information. That's why developing a plan of attack for dealing with the technology in your life is the best thing you can do to enhance your focus.

A study out of the University of San Francisco showed that rats could only make memories from a new experience if they had some downtime. Their brains need to be left undisturbed so that storage could take place. Another study, this time with humans, showed that people learned more after taking a walk in nature than if they walked around an urban environment before class. The University of Michigan researchers leading the study argued that urban environments are much more stimulating and therefore leave the brain with less downtime. Portable electronics like cell phones and laptops mimic this urban environment. They require so much cognitive energy that they can prevent the consolidation of new memories.

The way we interact with these devices is also changing the structure of our brains. You are probably familiar with the concept of plasticity in the brain, but here is a quick refresher. Neurons that fire together (*ie* are activated at the same time) tend to wire together (*ie* are more easily activated together the next time one or more gets triggered). If you are repeatedly shown a picture of an orange while someone says "naranja" to you (the Spanish word for orange), then in the future, when someone says naranja, you are likely to remember the image of the orange. Likewise, when you see the picture of the orange, the word naranja will probably come to mind. The neurons that encoded the word naranja and the neurons that encoded the picture of the orange were repeatedly fired together, so an association formed between them. They became 'wired' together. (We have a whole section on neuroplasticity coming later, so feel free to check that out if you need more details!)

Technology's effect on our brains is much more complicated than a simple link between a word and a picture. When we use devices, we tend to think we are 'multitasking' by simultaneously working on many things at once, but we are wrong. Perhaps we are checking Facebook while reading an article about homelessness, and also carrying out a text conversation with a friend, but we are never doing more than one thing at once. What we are actually doing is switching quickly between tasks. This task-switching changes our brain. A series of studies led by Eyal Ophir and others at Stanford University compared heavy 'multitasking' users of technology to more normal users of similar devices. They found that the multitaskers have more difficulty ignoring irrelevant information (*ie* they are more easily distracted). These multitaskers tend to always be anticipating new information, and this makes it difficult for them to use existing information to solve problems. How you interact with your devices causes changes in your brain that carry over to other aspects of your life. You may not think that you are losing much by giving yourself over to the immediate gratification of searching for new and interesting information, but there will be times in your life when you need to focus. Whether it's the standardized test that will decide at least part of your future, or a conversation with a friend you really care about, the ability to stay focused can really enrich your life.

But what can we do? In the developed world, being online, available and a user of these devices is nearly a requirement for living. A few of my friends have been able to survive without a cell phone, but only for short stints. I can't imagine life without an email address. You probably can't imagine doing homework without using Google. Ditching technology is not an option, but you have to develop a plan for using it responsibly, and a plan for healing your mind from its destructive effects.

Firstly, I would recommend turning off any sound effects that alert you of incoming messages on your cell phone and laptop. Sound cues can override even the most focused of minds, and you want to be the one in control of your technology, not the other way around. Schedule your email and text checks. Only check them when you have time to respond to them. Especially with emails; if you read them, and can respond in less than three minutes, just respond immediately. Do not let unfinished small tasks clutter your mind.

If you are worried about ignoring your friends when they text you, I would encourage you to think of times where they haven't responded to your messages. What has your response been? It is not the end of the world to respond later. If you are able to work on your schoolwork or other assignments in a more focused manner, you will be more efficient, and you will have more time to interact with them with your complete attention once you are done.

To protect and strengthen your mind, I recommend starting a mindfulness practice. Becoming comfortable with simply existing will allow your brain the downtime it needs in order to learn well. We have many sections on mindfulness, and I encourage you to start with Beginning Mindfulness.

Sources

Richtel, M. (2010). 'Growing up digital, wired for distraction'. *The New York Times*. www.nytimes.com/2010/11/21/technology/21brain.html?pagewanted=2&_r=1&

Richtel, M. (2010). 'Attached to technology and paying a price'. *The New York Times*. www.nytimes.com/2010/06/07/technology/07brain.html

Parker-Pope, T. (2010). 'The ugly toll of technology: impatience and forgetfulness.' *The New York Times*. www.nytimes.com/2010/06/07/technology/07brainside.html

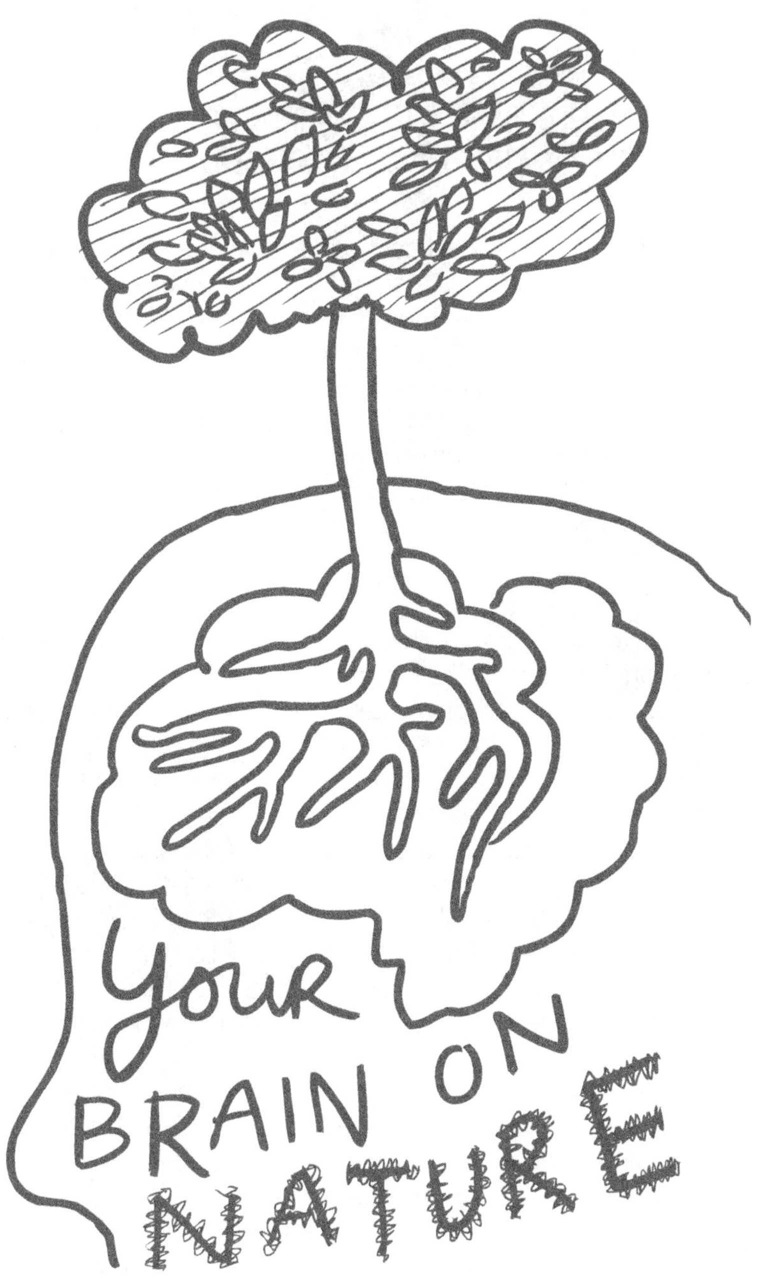
YOUR
BRAIN ON
NATURE

GET OUTSIDE: EFFECTS OF TECHNOLOGY ON OUR BRAINS PART II

As we talked about in the last section, our experiences are defined by screens. Large and small, shiny and matte, the glass-walled rectangles of our phones, laptops, televisions and tablets encourage us to look through them into the endless digital world. In doing so, we often neglect to spend time in the natural world, and that is a terrible mistake. A growing body of research shows that time spent outdoors, in forests, parks or on beaches can be an antidote to the stress, fractured attention span, and isolation we are induced to feel by the modern age.

Time spent in nature has been shown to make people more generous, relaxed and creative, but perhaps the most interesting research finding to date is how it can help regenerate our ability to focus. This research has roots in the work of late 1800s scientist William James. James famously (well, famously in the psychological community) conceived of two types of attention, voluntary and involuntary. You are exercising voluntary intention when you force yourself to pay attention in math class. The process takes effort, and you cannot do it indefinitely because you would get tired. The second kind of attention is what happens when something catches your attention. It could be an impromptu concert on a street corner, or the wind rustling the leaves in a tree. You do not have to exert any effort to pay attention, because the decision is not in your conscious control.

When we compare natural environments to urban environments, we can understand why nature might help restore our mental energy. When we are walking in the city, we have to be very aware of the dangers around us. Before we cross a street, we need to make sure that the light has changed. While there are many sights, sounds and smells that might capture our attention involuntarily, we need to wrestle this attention away in order to keep our mind on our tasks at hand. It is this struggle between voluntary and involuntary attention that can make urban environments exhausting. A similar dynamic is at play when we use media through screens. A computer offers many distractions, as does a phone. Pulling ourselves away from distractions requires use of our voluntary attention, which takes energy.

In a natural environment like a park, we can be much less concerned about immediate dangers and much more content to let our attention wander to where it has been drawn. Natural environments are full of textures and movements that fascinate us. We do not have to force ourselves to be present to these many small wonders, so our voluntary attention is allowed time to regenerate.

This theory explains why spending time in natural environments is so crucial. It provides us with the cognitive 'down-time' that is crucial for consolidating our learning. Spending time in a park is one of the cheapest and kindest things you can do for yourself. Even examining the blades of grass on your school's sports field will provide you with some of the benefits. Interacting with a natural place is a fantastic opportunity to be mindful. Focusing on the present moment is much easier when there are so many stimuli to draw your attention. You can look at how the light plays across the trunks of the trees, or watch flowers as they move slowly with the wind.

It sounds glib, but it's true: getting outside can make you stronger inside.

Sources

Todd, M. (2013). 'Is our disconnect from nature a disorder?'. *Pacific Standard*. www.psmag.com/nature-and-technology/nature-deficit-disorder-outdoors-outside-54707

McKinney, J. (2011). 'Thoreau was right: nature hones the mind'. *Pacific Standard*. www.psmag.com/nature-and-technology/put-down-the-ipad-lace-up-the-hiking-boots-51031

Kaplan, S. (1995). 'The restorative benefits of nature: towards an integrated framework'. *Journal of Environmental Psychology*. www.kon.org/urc/v11/thielen.html

zzzzz
SLEEP.

SLEEP AND NAPPING

The fact that human beings become immobile little snoring machines for one third of their lives is strange. No one can ever watch themselves sleep (except on video, but that would be a very boring video), but when you see other people sawing logs, you realize how strange sleep is. No one knows exactly why we need to sleep as much as we do, especially because not all animals sleep. What we do know is that cutting back on sleep is dangerous for ourselves and people around us (extreme tiredness has the same effects on our body as being drunk). Inadequate sleep decreases our cognitive speed and decision-making ability and increases our appetite and irritability. I doubt that any of this is news to you. You may also be aware that there are long-term consequences to poor sleep habits, such as an increased risk of chronic diseases like diabetes. And yet, when you ask yourself about your sleep habits, are you proud of them?

Research has shown that simply telling people about the negative consequences of their behaviour is not enough to convince them to change it, so in the rest of this section, I will work to explode all of the excuses you might have. You already know that sleep is good for you, but here's why you can easily get the sleep you need.

If you think you are too busy to get enough sleep, think again. You are probably working much less efficiently because of your constantly sleep-deprived state. Take a holiday from a few of your commitments so that you can get a handle on your sleep patterns, and then slowly add things back to your plate. Be honest with others about your health concerns, and they will likely accommodate you.

If you try to go to sleep at a reasonable time and find yourself unable to drift off, you could have a few different issues. The first is that you are not sufficiently tired. This is an easy problem to fix! Physical activity can do wonders for your ability to sleep. Read our section on the Case For Exercise for some ideas about how to incorporate more activity into your life.

The second issue is created by the electronic screens that surround us. If you use laptops and cell phones just before bed, you are sapping your body's ability to produce melatonin, a hormone that is important for triggering sleepy feelings. The blue light produced by these electronic devices is particularly harmful for melatonin production. One solution is to leave your devices out of your bedroom, but if you can't bear the thought of that, there is a free application called f.lux (www.justgetflux.com) that changes the colour of the light of your screen based on the time of the day. As night draws closer, your screen becomes more orange. I have used it for years and notice the difference.

If you find that you are anxious about incomplete tasks, and that this is preventing you from falling asleep easily, develop a night time ritual where you write down all that needs to be done. Thoughts of incomplete tasks tend to intrude into our consciousness (as you might have read about in our section about organizing your mind), but writing them down will give you the peace of mind that they are stored somewhere, allowing you to relax and focus on sleeping.

A weird-sounding tip that I find very helpful is to try to force yourself to stay awake. So long as you are not hitting yourself or putting ice in your shirt, telling yourself that you need to stay awake and trying to do so can actually help you nod off. Why? It may reduce your anxiety. Trying to fall asleep and being unable to do so is frustrating and may unsettle you. If you tell yourself that your goal is to stay awake, you release some of that anxiety.

Finally, if you find yourself getting tired in the afternoon, there is nothing wrong with having a 20 minute nap. In fact, naps of this length have been shown to significantly enhance your creativity and cognitive speed. Be careful not to sleep for too long (30 minutes plus), or else you might be very groggy and nauseous when you wake up, because you will have entered a deeper phase of your sleep cycle.

Hopefully these little tips have removed all of the reasons you had for not getting enough sleep. You deserve to be well rested, so don't waste any more time pretending that you don't.

Sources

N.a. (2009). 'To go to sleep, try to stay awake'. *Sleep Education Blog.* The American Academy of Sleep Medicine. www.sleepeducation.blogspot.ca/2009/01/to-go-to-sleep-try-to-stay-awake.html

N.a. (2012). 'Blue light has a dark side'. *Harvard Health Letter.* Harvard Medical School. www.health.harvard.edu/staying-healthy/blue-light-has-a-dark-side

Henry, A. (2012). 'The science behind why power naps help you stay productive and creative'. *Lifehacker.* www.lifehacker.com/5932754/the-science-behind-why-power-naps-help-you-stay-productive-and-creative

Fryer, B. (2006). 'Sleep deficit: the performance killer'. *Harvard Business Review.* www.hbr.org/2006/10/sleep-deficit-the-performance-killer

the CASE for EXERCISE

THE CASE FOR EXERCISE

Banish cringe-inducing memories of gym class, because exercise is one of the best things you can do for yourself. Human beings did not evolve to sit in front of computers. We evolved to roam savannahs in search of food, and to run to evade predators. Mountains of research papers have been published that link regular physical exercise to all kinds of health benefits. Being active can help you sleep, improve your mood, extend your lifespan, make you more productive, and reduce your stress level. Doctors have even begun to issue specific 'prescriptions' for exercise, in hopes of increasing the health of their patients. Yet so many of us don't do it. We know all of the benefits, but we don't stick to our commitment to be physical. Why does this happen and what can we do about it?

The first problem is that people tend to focus on the wrong outcomes. Often, we may start to exercise because we want to get in shape and/or lose weight. Making progress on these two goals by exercise alone takes a long time. When we don't see results right away, we get discouraged and give up. Focusing on the immediate benefits of exercise, especially the great feeling we get after a workout, is a better choice, because it helps us build the habit of exercising, and makes it more likely that we will stick with our activities long enough to enjoy the long-term benefits as well.

The second issue is that people think of exercise too narrowly. Most often, they think of it as something that needs to happen in a gym, on a treadmill, or on a field. Our days are actually rife with opportunities to be physically active. Taking the stairs at school rather than the elevator, going for a walk at lunch, or biking to pick up groceries are all examples of exercise. People also think that exercise needs to be unpleasant, but this belief leads them to choose activities that they don't enjoy and will likely not stick to. Exercise should be fun and rewarding. It is important to challenge our bodies and get our lungs working, but if you are trying to build a habit of exercise, it is a terrible idea to start with punishing workouts. Try to aim for a Goldilocks level – not too easy, not too hard. Err on the side of too easy rather than too hard. Gradually increasing the intensity of your exercise will prevent you from being overwhelmed and quitting.

The third issue is that people do not plan well enough for their exercise. You can learn about this in our section on System 1 and System 2, it is very important to use our deliberative thinking to anticipate and shape our behaviour when we go into automatic mode. One tactic I have used many times is to print out the fitness class schedule of my gym and decide which classes fit into my days. Once I have decided which classes I will go to, I ensure that I have my gym bag ready the night before. Essentially, I decide for my future self that I will go to the gym, and make it as easy as possible for my future self to carry out these directives.

Fourth, and finally, people decide to take on this challenge alone. Involving other people in your plans can help you past obstacles. Whether you do so by going to group fitness classes, where you can be motivated by the efforts of others, or by inviting a friend along for a bike ride, if there is a way to find allies in your quest to reap the benefits of exercise, I suggest that you do it.

Sources

Weir, K. (2011). 'The exercise effect'. *The Monitor.* American Psychological Association. www.apa.org/monitor/2011/12/exercise.aspx

Andrews, L. (2014). 'Why is it so hard to exercise?'. *Raising Fit Kids.* Web MD and Sanford Health. www.webmd.com/parenting/raising-fit-kids/move/motivated-to-exercise?page=3

N.a. (2013). 'Doctors writing prescriptions to get patients active'. *CBC News Health.* www.cbc.ca/news/health/doctors-writing-prescriptions-to-get-patients-active-1.1355824

THERAPEUTIC
STACKING

THERAPEUTIC STACKING

Most of you are probably wary of multitasking, as you should be. Multitasking really means constantly switching between two different tasks, and often means that you perform both of them poorly. Stacking is not multitasking. If it feels that way, you are doing it wrong. What you are aiming for when you are stacking is simultasking. You should not be conscious of switching back and forth between the tasks (or these switches should happen very rarely).

Most pairs of tasks can't be simultasked, but there is a subset of ones that can be combined easily with other tasks. They tend to be physical tasks you are quite familiar with. That's right, chores! Cooking, cleaning, and even moderate exercise all fall into this category. These domains of your life do not have to be boredom-inducing. They can be ways for you to fully engage in your life, and at the same time recharge yourself and your environment. Think of it as therapeutic stacking.

You can wash dishes and listen to music. You can sweep the floors and listen to a podcast. You can even clean your room and meditate. You can chop carrots and talk to a friend (be careful with sharp objects!). You can go on a hike with your brother. In all of these cases, you have made time for additional learning, entertainment, mental health or social interaction, and you have done so by doubling it up with a task that is essential for your physical and/or mental well-being. You have added time to your schedule by mixing play and work. You may even start to do the unthinkable – love chores! Well done!

Therapeutic stacking is an example of recognizing an unexploited opportunity in your day, and using this opportunity to enhance your ability to care for yourself. It is an act of love for you and others.

WILLPOWER
&
FOOD
=
BFFLS

WILLPOWER AND FOOD

For one glorious semester in my second year of university, I enjoyed what I called "lunch and a show." I would take my lunch to my multi-variable calculus class, and in between furiously annotating equations, I would enjoy spoonfuls of applesauce and stew (I liked to use my slow-cooker, so many of my foods had the same texture). What started as a decision born of convenience (the class spanned my normal lunch hour) soon became a survival mechanism. I found that without the steady stream of snacks, I could not focus on the scores of chalk-drawn symbols on the board. Initially, I thought that the food was allowing me to comfort myself as I struggled to understand what was being taught, but I slowly noticed that I would use food in other academic situations as well. Writing a research paper required multiple visits to the fridge to choose apples and yogurt. Reading difficult passages from a philosophy textbook required celery. Instead of just quelling my anxieties, I began to suspect that I was fuelling my brain.

Because of this suspicion, I was not surprised when I read that while our brains make up only three percent of our body weight, they consume one quarter of the glucose that circulates in our blood. It makes sense. We don't often think about the fact that our brains are made of cells just like the rest of our bodies, but they are. Think of all the electrical impulses that need to travel throughout your grey and white matter! Think of all the ion pumps that need fuel to function. Your brain is a fantastically hungry machine.

Knowing that our brain needs fuel to function helps us understand why willpower and self control are depletable resources. If you burn up your glucose trying to withstand the temptation of potato chips at the cafeteria, you might find that you don't have the energy to convince yourself to go to the gym after school. Researchers have found that if they give a task that requires willpower (abstaining from eating cookies) to students, they perform worse on a problem-solving test than students who did not have to control themselves.

Understanding how your brain works can help you make better choices. There are two approaches you can take to ensure that your willpower and focus is there when you need it. The first is an immediate fix, while the second is a systemic fix that requires more up-front effort. I would recommend both! (This approach is aligned with our section on System 1 and System 2).

The first approach is to mimic my behavior in math class and keep yourself supplied with (hopefully healthy) snacks. When you are feeling brain-tired or foggy, try to reach for some carrots rather than immediately throwing in the towel. A snack and a cold glass of water can do wonders for your morale and your mental energy. Crunchy snacks with lots of water and a bit of sugar (apples, carrots, and celery, for example) are wonderful options. You might even want to label a "Brain Food" container and put it in your fridge, in order to make it really easy to make good snacking choices when you are glucose-low.

The second approach is to try to remove the need for willpower from many of your daily activities. Try to automate your wardrobe by choosing clothes the night before. Take some time on Sunday to plan your exercise, extracurriculars and school work. The goal of this approach is to make your daily decision-making more streamlined (all you have to do is follow your plan). The caveat to this approach is that it can make you feel a little robotic. A remedy for this caveat is to find a rewarding, human and creative way to use the time and energy you gain from making better choices (perhaps exploring your city, or cooking exotic dishes). Of course, there is nothing wrong with juggling your schedule around to take advantage of arising opportunities. Having a good plan usually means that you will be able to judge whether you have time for a movie with your cousin, or to make dinner for your parents, as we've discussed in our sections about organization.

A mixture of both approaches is probably best. Conserving your mental energy (our second recommended approach) is only effective to a point. You can't avoid thinking entirely (nor should you!). It is important to understand what is happening when your brain feels tired, because it helps you realize how much control you really do have over your mental state. Remember, if you feel beat, make time to eat!

Sources

Sapolsky, R. (2014). 'How the brain uses glucose to fuel self-control.' *Wall Street Journal*. www.wsj.com/articles/how-the-brain-uses-glucose-to-fuel-self-control-1417618996

Dutton, J. (2012). 'Conserve your willpower: it runs out'. *WIRED*. www.wired.com/2012/10/mf-willpower

FINDING YOUR PATH

NOT JUST PASSION

Have you ever thought about what would happen if everyone in the world dropped what they were doing and pursued their "passions"? I think we would have a world overrun with doctors, teachers, movie stars, bakery owners, fashion designers, and writers. Now, this experiment can never really be performed, but I am confident in the outcome I predict because of a cognitive quirk that we all share. It is called the availability bias.

Here is an example of the availability bias in action. You have been seeing advertisements for a new brand of cookie all over your town. You decide to shop for groceries, and when you reach the cookie aisle and are trying to decide between all of the different delicious options, you decide to give this new brand a try. Instead of considering all of the possible options, your brain looks for what is the most available. What does it mean for something to be available? It is easier to access than other information. Either you have recently been exposed to this information, (so it is already partially 'activated' in your mind), or it is vivid and easy to remember (perhaps the logo of the cookie is a cute puppy). The availability heuristic is one of the reasons why you see lawn signs during elections. The candidates want their names to be familiar once you get to the ballot box!

The availability heuristic is a mental shortcut. Most of the time, it helps us make decent decisions quickly. When you run downstairs, but then forget what it was you were trying to find, the availability heuristic helps you zero in on the few items it could be (what was in the back of your mind) so that you can avoid going through all the items in your basement as if they were on a big list. Still, there are many scenarios in which the most obvious option is not the best answer. Envisioning yourself in a career is a crucial example. Many of your classmates, and perhaps even you, have thought about certain careers, but have you ever wondered why certain ones appealed to you over all of the other possibilities? My guess is that perhaps someone in your family has that job, or you have watched a television series about the profession (especially if it is something related to medicine), or you have read about a person with that profession. In short, you may be interested in certain fields because they are more available to you than others, but availability alone doesn't mean that they are the right choices for you. For one thing, careers that are profiled in popular culture are going to be more available to everyone, so there will be more competition. You may have to put in more effort than you would in another field to get the same reward. Also, the reasons that cause certain careers to be profiled in the media do not always overlap with factors that will make them satisfying. There are a lot of burned-out, overworked and bored detectives, lawyers and doctors.

There is nothing wrong with aspiring to be a doctor, laywer, pop superstar or detective, of course. I would just caution you to examine your motives for pursuing these popular, competitive or traditional paths. Are they based in logic, or do they spring from what is familiar? Any career that can provide you with the chance to have control over how and what you work on, the opportunity to build valuable skills, and the chance to feel connected to a team or community is one that can be satisfying. There are thousands of paths that are not immediately obvious, but just because they are not 'available' does not mean that they hold no promise.

Even if you are thinking of a traditional path, I would encourage you to consider a few alternative options. What is it about these careers that you admire? Is it the recognition you might get from the public? Being able to write? Having work topics that change frequently? Once you have isolated these elements, try to think of a few other professions where they can also be found. You don't have to change your life plans, but you should at least put them in context, to make sure your desires are grounded in something real.

Sources

Cherry, K. 'Availability heuristic.' *About Psychology*. www.psychology.about.com/od/aindex/g/availability-heuristic.htm

Dean, J. (2012). 'The availability bias: why people buy lottery tickets.' *PsyBlog*. www.spring.org.uk/2012/08/the-availability-bias-why-people-buy-lottery-tickets.php

Newport, C. (2009). 'Are passions serendipitously discovered or painstakingly constructed?'. *Study Hacks Blog: Decoding Patterns of Success*. www.calnewport.com/blog/2009/11/24/are-passions-serendipitously-discovered-or-painstakingly-constructed/

All you need is
AUTONOMY
&
MASTERY
&
PURPOSE
1

FINDING YOUR PATH PART II

Determining what to do with your life, or even the first little chunk of your life, is an important and often intimidating task. As we explored in our first section on passion, sometimes we aspire to be what we most frequently see, but these highly 'available' careers (re-read that section if you're confused by this reference to the availability bias) are only a slim slice of what's available.

Have you ever considered becoming a bank teller, software quality assurance engineer, executive chef, property manager, warehouse manager or administrative assistant? These occupations aren't ones normally profiled on television, except perhaps through tongue-in-cheek shows such as *The Office*, but you might be surprised to learn that they topped out the rankings when more than 100,000 employees were asked to rate their jobs. The fact that these top six seem relatively ordinary underscores the idea that factors other than passion should be considered when we are thinking about satisfaction and success.

Daniel Pink reviewed 50 years of behavioural science research when he was preparing to write a book about motivation. In a TED talk he gave on the same topic, he notes that the three crucial elements of any motivating or satisfying job are autonomy, mastery and purpose. All three seem like common-sense findings. Of course, people would want to have some level of control over the work they do; no one likes being bossed around all the time. Of course, as well, people tend to enjoy things if they are able to perform them at a high level of skill. And, finally, of course people want to feel as though their contributions are meaningful, whether to their work team, their customers, or even the world.

Many careers can offer you all three of these elements, but it is important to remember that it might not all happen at once. Why would you be given any autonomy if you haven't proved yourself capable? How can you become a master at something you were just introduced to a few weeks ago? Especially when you are working on your own, learning and trying to understand the system or organization you are planning on joining, you might feel like there is very little purpose to what you are doing.

My first 'real' job was spent working in a medical research lab. As I wrote in the introduction, I had to dissolve mouse tails in acid and extract their DNA. While I enjoyed the autonomy with which I was allowed to work, and the mastery I was slowly but surely gaining, the purpose element was missing. I understood the focus of the research in which the lab was engaged, but I did not feel like it really mattered (at least not to me). To change this feeling, I could have tried harder to understand the potential implications of the research, but I did not. I reasoned to myself that it was just a summer job. I was wrong. I owed it to myself to make that experience as satisfying as I could. Knowing what I do now, I would have tried to understand how I fit into the lab a little better. I could have asked myself to consider whose research was I helping when I was dissolving those mouse tails? How might it help them finish their graduate work or become a professor?

What do these paragraphs all boil down to? If you don't have a defined passion, don't despair. There are many pathways to a rewarding career. However, these inroads and pathways need to be found by you! They likely won't be handed to you. So long as you keep in mind autonomy, mastery and purpose, you will be able to jump from opportunity to opportunity with good reason, accumulating more of these elements as you go.

Knowing that you can find autonomy, mastery, and purpose in many careers might allow you to think about other factors that will influence a good fit. Certain personalities are better suited for roles that require a lot of social interaction. Are you one of those people? I know that I am not. Other types of careers will keep you isolated most of the time. Is this what makes you the most comfortable? It could be the sign of a good fit. Aspects of your personality can take a while to change, so often it is best to work with them rather than against them. Try to find roles where your characteristics are seen as assets and not liabilities.

Still, often it's not just about the work, but also the context in which you are working. We'll delve more into this person-context fit in part III of this section.

Sources

Pink, D. (2009). 'The puzzle of motivation'. *TED Global 2009.* www.ted.com/talks/dan_pink_on_motivation/transcript?language=en

Smith, J. (2012). 'The happiest jobs in America'. *Forbes.* www.forbes.com/sites/jacquelynsmith/2012/03/23/the-happiest-jobs-in-america/

FINDING
your
WHEN
WHERE
HOW
f(x)
WITH
WHO
WHY
WHAT
FIT

FINDING YOUR PATH III

When people try to picture themselves in different careers, they tend to focus on the tasks they will be performing while on the job. Medical hopefuls imagine themselves seeing patients. Engineering wannabes think of stress-testing a bike helmet. However, when you think of some of the best or worst experiences you've had, can you find examples where you had an incredible time engaged in a routine task, or a terrible time engaged in a really interesting task? Maybe throwing a ball back and forth, outside, with your friend was so much more enjoyable than watching a new movie all by yourself. These tasks do not exist in a vacuum. When you are considering what careers might fit you well, it is important to consider the context of your work as well as the work itself.

Perhaps you already know that staying close to your family is important to you. If you live in the middle of a landlocked city and you have dreams of being an oceanographer, chances are you will have to make a compromise. If you love the city in which you are living, but have only vague ideas about what you would like to do after school, understanding the major industries of your hometown could help you narrow your list of options. Perhaps you want to end up in the sunny climes of California, in which case learning computer programming would be a good bet. The moral of this story? Think carefully. There is more to a job than what it is; where it is also matters.

You might be in a land of endless sun, but if you dread interacting with your collaborators, your life will not be enjoyable, and you will not be performing at your full potential. What you do is important, but so is who you will be doing it with, and how you will be interacting with them. Pay attention to stereotypes about different professions. While they likely exaggerate, there is usually a nugget of truth in them. Certain professions, like accounting, require an exacting attention to detail and for their practitioners to adhere closely to rules. Other professions, such as nursing, tend to draw in people who are very empathic. Still others, like corporate law, tend to draw people who are highly ambitious. When you are trying to understand where your fit lies, consider the kinds of people you will be working beside. Do their broad personality traits (attention to detail, level of stress, extraversion) match with those you already have or wish to develop?

Realize as well that you do not have to feel as though you are making a 50 year commitment when you decide on a profession. You will be quite a different person 20 years from now than you are currently, and you may develop other interests that will shift your path. In the business world, this is called 'pivoting'. When you pivot, you try to look at your skills and experiences objectively, and then imagine a new context in which you could better use them. Perhaps a doctor could use her experience with patients to become an excellent playwright. It is impossible to know how your working life will unfold. Still, trying to optimize for fit when it comes to your first choice will help you stay working long enough to build good, transferable skills that can give you the option of pivoting when the time comes.

Sources

Spoon, A. (2012). 'What 'pivot' really means'. *Pivot: Reinvention Central.* Inc. www.inc.com/alan-spoon/what-pivot-really-means.html

FIND
BLUE OCEANS

BLUE OCEAN STRATEGY: FINDING YOUR PATH IV

Let's say you are trying to create a computer program that can beat a normal person at chess. How could you do it? One idea would be to list every possible set of moves the human opponent could make, and then figure out how the computer could respond. Even from the description, it seems like it would take a long time, but I don't think you fully appreciate how long this would take. The number of possible combinations of moves is mind-boggling. Edward Tsang of the University of Essex has calculated that in order to consider what might happen 15 moves ahead in a chess game, a computer would have to calculate for 90 million hours! What's to blame? A phenomenon called combinatorial explosion. Essentially, for certain problems, the difficulty of solving them by trial and error increases exponentially as the problem size increases linearly. A simple example is trying to guess someone's password. If it is only two letters, you have 26 possibilities for the first letter, and 26 possibilities for the second letter, so the total number of items you have to check is 676. If there are four letters, you have over 45,000 combinations to check. The problem has gotten only twice as large, but your difficulty of solving it has increased by more than 600 times! Combinatorial explosion is one of the thorniest problems in computing, but you might be wondering why it is a problem for you.

Combinatorial explosion reminds us that there are a vast number of possibilities for important combinations in our lives. The combination we will focus on in this section is the combination of traits, locations and tasks that make up your career. You could be a orthopedic surgeon in Paris, or a small claims adjustor in Toronto. You could be an art therapist working at a hospital in Chicago, or own a convenience store near Bath. These are all glamorous examples, but the point is, you have many options. Unless you are someone who was born with a deadset intention towards a particular career, there are many options that will probably fit you, how you want to live, and what you want to achieve.

Assuming that you are in the second group, the group of kids who was born without any deadset intentions, I have an idea to share with you. It comes from Renee Marbourgne and W. Chan Kim, two researchers at the INSEAD School of Business. They found that while most companies tend to fight it out in 'red oceans', market spaces made bloody by so much competition, the few mavericks who think creatively and find 'blue oceans' for themselves can attain much larger success. What are these 'blue oceans'? They are the spaces that no one else has claimed; they are opportunities that have not been sensed by other firms. Instead of spending most of their energy fighting with others to solve the same problems for the same people, these firms channel their effort into creative thinking. They find other people and new problems to solve.

You are not a company, I know, but if you are not too tied to a particular path, I think that adopting this mindset when you think about your career can be very fruitful. If you have an area of interest, whether it is education, health care, finance, biology or music (or anything else you like!), try to map out the current 'system'. What kinds of organizations exist currently? Where are they falling short? How can you train yourself to become the kind of person that can help others open up 'blue oceans'? It is not enough to have a single focus. You need to have a strong set of skills that are complemented by knowledge and experience in another field. If you are interested in psychiatry, for example, studying novels alongside neuroscience might help you develop the first literary psychiatry practice in the world. If you are interested in international development, learning about different financial models and economic systems may allow you to figure out how to make development efforts financially sustainable. If you want to be a writer, build your illustration skills at the same time. Your school paper will be more likely to publish your work if it comes with a hand-drawn infographic.

Instead of trying to compete with others, vault over them into a niche that fits your interests, experiences and personality. Use your energy to create and enhance your own skills rather than spending it trying to outdo someone else. The way to win is to rise above the game.

Sources

Marbourgne, R. and Kim, W. (2005). *Blue ocean strategy: how to create uncontested market space and make the competition irrelevant.* Harvard Business Review Press: New York.

Marbourgne, R. and Kim, W. (2004). 'Blue ocean strategy'. *Harvard Business Review.* www.hbr.org/2004/10/blue-ocean-strategy

Tsang, E. (2005). 'Combinatorial explosion'. *Tutorials.* Constraint Satisfaction and Optimization Group, University of Essex. http://cswww.essex.ac.uk/CSP/finance/ComputationalFinanceTeaching/CombinatorialExplosion.html

STACK YOUR

FULFIL THE REQUIREMENTS

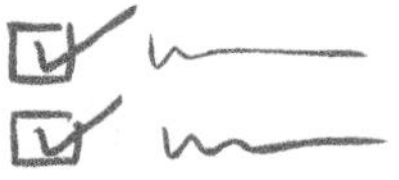

BUILD SKILLS

MEET COOL PEOPLE

CAS HOURS

FIND YOUR PATH WITH CAS

As an IB student, you are probably very familiar with the CAS acronym. Perhaps the 50 hours each of creativity, action and service in which you are expected to engage makes you feel intimidated. We both know how heavy your academic workload is, and you are also probably wondering about your future options. What should you study? What kind of career should you be stepping towards? How can you manage all three of these tasks?

One solution is to stack the task of exploring your future options on top of the task of completing your CAS hours. See the hours you are required to spend as an opportunity rather than an obligation. You can use this time to engage more deeply in different interests of yours, and meet and help inspiring people. A benefit of youth, one that you might not realize until you are older, is that people are often willing to help you. When you are a student, often all that you need to do in order to get people to offer you informational interviews is to tell them that you are a student, and that you are interested in what they do for a living, or, even, that you would like to help with the festival that they are organizing. Seeing the word 'student' often prompts people to think of their own youth, and they tend to project these warm feelings onto you. Moreover, having a CAS hour requirement gives you an even more official reason to talk to them. Depending on your interests, any combination of your creativity, action and service hours can be stacked with other tasks. Let's move through the different sections and discuss some simple examples for each one.

Creativity hours can be used to give you a taste of what working in a few areas of your interest might be like. Creativity can be found in more areas than just the arts (but if that is where your talents and interest lies, by all means, write, dance, sing, draw, or emote!). You can be creative while designing assistive cardboard devices for people with special needs (while testing your interest in engineering), writing an article about recent advances in neuroscience (a task which would allow you to interview different university-level researchers), or even creating a website for a non-profit organization (building your computer skills along the way). While these creative pursuits can be done with minimal supervision, I would advise looking for ways to partner with others. Combining volunteering with creative pursuits can also be a great way to challenge yourself to learn and practice new skills, because knowing that you have an external partner who needs and will appreciate the results of your work is a strong motivating factor. So long as you do not take on an impossible challenge (you need to respect the time and effort the organization is putting into maintaining this relationship with you), you can help improve yourself while making a difference for others. Moreover, you will often be able to get feedback on the quality of your work, which can help you accurately assess your strengths and locate your blind spots. Whenever you create something you are proud of, add it to your CV or portfolio, as this is a great way to show your interests and talents to others. Volunteering with a few friends who have similar interests can also allow you to stay motivated and enjoy the often hard work that defines the creative process.

When it comes to action, unless your goal is to find a place in a profession that involves movement or fitness, things will probably be simpler. Engage in activities you enjoy, and reap the many benefits of exercise. Service, on the other hand, is another domain that is ripe for stacking. So long as you keep the ultimate goal of serving others in mind, there is nothing wrong with choosing activities that also serve you in some way. In fact, finding situations where there is mutual gain will help you to be more motivated and to engage more fully. If you are interested in law, for example, you might be able to volunteer at a non-profit community legal center, and interact with lawyers as well as their clients. If you are interested in entrepreneurship, perhaps there is a mentorship organization that connects fledgling CEOs with experienced executives, and they might even need your help. If you have defined interests, do a little bit of digging to see whether there is a way to serve the community while testing your assumptions about a path you might like to pursue.

Seeing your CAS hours as an opportunity to develop yourself as well as a requirement to be filled is a small change in perspective that can lead to 150 hours of much more enjoyable, rewarding and meaningful engagement – for you and for others.

Sources

N.a. (2015). 'Creativity, activity, service'. *Diploma Programme.* International Baccalaureate.www.ibo.org/en/programmes/diploma-programme/curriculum/creativity-action-and-service/

NARRATIVES

NARRATIVES are LIFE SIMULATORS

NARRATIVES AS LIFE SIMULATORS

Life is a poorly designed experiment. If you have learned anything about experimental design, you know that it is important to have multiple trials so that you can ensure the results you obtained on the first one weren't just due to error or chance. You also know that it is very important to have 'control' groups where you have changed nothing, so that you know if your condition makes a real difference.

Now, think about your life. Reproducing your results might be possible when you are cooking, but for big life decisions (*eg* where to attend school, what career path to aspire to, how to interact with others in high school), you only get one chance. Moreover, you cannot compare your choices to a control, because there is only one of you! Even if you examine what happens to those around you, there is still a problem: you are always racing into the future. If you see a difference between the results of their choices and your choice, by the time you decide to change your course, time will have passed and the scenario will be different. Let's make this more concrete. What if you graduated from high school without taking math and physics courses, and you see that your friends who did take those courses were able to apply for engineering programs at university? You would observe that different choices led to different results, but would that learning be actionable? If you are willing to complete another few years of high school, perhaps it would. Often, though, we don't have the option of a do-over.

What can you do if you do want to be able to learn from the choices of others? You simply have to solve the tiny problem of time passing! Stumped? I have two suggestions for you. You can choose to learn about things that have already happened, or things that have never really happened at all. The first is perhaps easier to defend, so we will start there. All you need to do is become a student of history.

Though many aspects of your present environment may be different, when it comes to the big choices in life, you are not the first human being to have grappled with any of them. In fact, you come from a long line of grapplers. There is much to learn from turning backwards. The easiest people to learn from are probably people in your family. Older siblings are useful because their experiences are still fresh. They will understand your context better than people who are older. Still, they have not had as much time to reflect on their choices, or to see the consequences of their decisions unfold. Your parents and grandparents can share a longer-term view. They can put your questions about a particular decision into a broader context full of many other large decisions they have had to make.

Listening to these narratives does not guarantee that you will repeat the successes and avoid the mistakes of their pasts. Our memories are notoriously fallible. Sometimes the story we tell ourselves about what happened can overwrite the facts. People also have a tendency, called hindsight bias, to describe events as if they were much more predictable than they seemed at the time. Your grandmother might tell you that she never should have agreed to leave high school, because she would never get another chance to be educated, but she is speaking from her position in the future rather than putting herself in her own shoes from 60 years ago. It is important to remember that whatever stories you are being told are simplified and skewed, but that does not mean they are useless. The particulars of these experiences might not match up to your own, but the general themes should ring true. Perhaps your parents gave up their dreams and feel bittersweet about their life experiences. Perhaps your siblings wish they had been more social or grateful. You have an opportunity to act on their knowledge. Having these conversations also gives you a chance to deepen your bonds with your family. It reminds you that everyone around you has a story you can learn from.

Of course, you should not feel limited to your immediate family circle. Memoirs of people with extraordinary lives, storytelling radio podcasts, and news reports can all give you glimpses into the lives of others who have made certain choices. The diversity of stories is crucial, because you are looking for truths that seem to unite them. Learning from other people who are separated from you in time and space can help you feel more in control of your own life. Because you have more experimental results, you become wiser. You can turn the odds more in your favour by refusing to see your life as a poorly designed experiment. I wish you luck!

Sources

Cherry, K. (2015) 'Hindsight bias.' *About Psychology*. www.psychology.about.com/od/hindex/g/hindsight-bias.htm

ART IS LIFE
LEARN FROM IT

WHY READ LITERATURE?

Books matter. It's true – reading fiction can enrich your life and your choices. A study led by researcher Maja Djikic at the University of Toronto showed that reading short passages of fiction helped people become more comfortable with uncertainty, and reduced their likelihood of making hasty or 'snap' decisions (compared to people who read non-fiction, or nothing at all). Previous studies by the same team showed that readers of fiction were more empathetic towards others than non-readers were.

Djikic argues that although we care about the characters we encounter in novels and short stories (allowing us to practice our empathy), the gap between reader and character is never fully closed. This distance allows us to feel safe and calm even while we are reading about the messiness and chaos of their lives. We have a front-row seat to complicated situations, and we can spend our time trying to understand them. When we are faced with these situations in our own lives, we might not feel so overwhelmed.

Films can also increase our ability to empathize on multiple levels. When neuroscience researcher Talma Hendler examined the changes in brain activity that occurred while volunteers watched the movie *Black Swan*, she noticed that two types of empathy were happening. The first was visceral empathy. If a character was cut, the audience felt a dimmer version of this sensation. The second was what we might call 'analytical' empathy, and occurred when the audience was trying to understand what the character was thinking or feeling. This type of empathy is a skill that needs to be practiced. Movies and books can act as a great training ground.

Still, what does being able to empathize have to do with making better choices in your life? Having a better understanding of other people (what their body language might suggest, or how their experiences may have shaped them) will allow you to make choices about the people with whom you choose to spend time. It will also help you accomplish all aspects of your plans that involve interacting with others. Narratives, whether in film, print or otherwise, often allow us to access the rich inner worlds of other people. One of the loneliest things about being a conscious human being, at least in my opinion, is having no way to share exactly what is occurring in your mind with others. We also have a tendency, as people, to assume that we are the main character in our story, and that other people must have less vibrant or less important experiences than us. Engaging with these narratives reminds us that every single person is the main character of their own journey. Just as we view them as supporting characters, they view us as people with only minor roles to play in their own drama.

Realizing that other people are just as human and interesting as we are can lead us to take their challenges, choices, and accumulated wisdom more seriously. We have much to learn from exposing ourselves to other people, even if they are characters who were dreamed up in a writer's room in sunny and smoggy Los Angeles.

A character's story does not need to be true to be useful. Often, our reaction to characters tells us a great deal about our own values. Our own assumptions shape every choice we make, but can be hard to surface. Reflecting on our reactions to these narratives gives us a chance to piece together what our values must be. For example, if you were very upset by a father's decision to place workplace success on a higher level than his relationship with his daughter, you might value flexibility and belonging more than the material trappings of success. Unearthing these values does not mean you have to feel trapped by them. Identifying them is the first step towards understanding where they came from and whether you would like to question or change them. We will dig further into this issue when we come to our Surfacing Assumptions section.

Until then, do not deny yourself entrance into the rich inner worlds of fictional characters. You can see yourself and your circumstances reflected in them. You can transcend the limitations of your body and assimilate your experiences with theirs. Reading or watching films can allow you to sample many more paths than is possible in normal life. Just like understanding the 'true to life' stories of those around you, following fictional storylines can help you build a context for yourself. When hard times come, you will be more likely to greet them with understanding rather than with surprise. When tough decisions need to be made, you might find yourself remembering others who have stood at similar crossroads, and while these memories might not show you the way, they can help you feel more prepared for whatever lies down the road you choose.

Sources

Harris, M. (2013). 'Reading literary fiction can lead to better decision-making, new study finds'. *National Post*. http://news.nationalpost.com/arts/books/reading-literary-fiction-can-lead-to-an-better-decision-making-study-finds

Miller, G. (2014). 'How movies trick your brain into empathizing with characters'. *WIRED*. www.wired.com/2014/09/cinema-science-empathizing-with-characters/

YOUR
ME
STORY
BECOMES
YOUR
REALITY

THE STORIES WE TELL

Constellations are stories made of stars. Thousands of years ago, people looked into the night sky and made sense of the random distribution of points of light among the darkness. They saw bears, hunters, swans, and mythical creatures. Human beings are primed to see patterns, even those that occur randomly. We are meaning-making machines. We use patterns and stories to explain our world, our lives, and ourselves.

Any story is a simplification. It is almost the same as drawing a line between a few stars in the night sky. Some points of fact must be left out. Others need to be supplied or imagined. A story passes judgment. It has a perspective because otherwise it would not be quite so easy to follow. A good story traces a path we can follow, allowing us to make a messy topic coherent.

One of the messiest topics I think you will ever encounter is yourself. You are a collection of memories, tendencies, opinions, reactions, thoughts, dreams, and fears. To understand yourself, you engage in storytelling. You select certain pieces of information about yourself and string them into a story. This story is your identity, but it also shapes your identity. Understanding yourself in a certain way influences your future actions. If you think of yourself as adventurous, you might look for adventures on which to embark. If you think of yourself as fantastic at mathematics, you will likely explain away a bad result as accidental. The stories you tell about your past have a subtle way of shaping your future.

Researcher Jonathan Adler studied the stories people tell about themselves, or 'personal narratives', for his doctorate degree at the University of Waterloo. He found that people who are mentally healthy and positive tend to tell certain types of stories about themselves. These stories might start out bad – perhaps someone breaks her leg, or loses his job – but they tend to have happy endings.

The people telling them tend to choose to focus on what they learned from the experience, or what good things happened to them as an indirect result of the negative event occurring. Adler calls these redemption stories. You might be wondering whether people who are happier and more mentally healthy just tended to have fewer terrible things happen to them, but Adler disputes this idea. He has seen very similar life events - divorce, for example - narrated in different ways. Interpretation matters more than the facts of an event. There will always be so many direct and indirect consequences to choose from.

Adler has found that people can be trained to tell better stories about themselves. Through practice, people can learn to see themselves as a strong main character, rather than a passive victim. This understanding shapes their actions, which eventually shapes their destiny.

Negative stories can damage us. Unless we challenge them, by actively seeking another interpretation of an event, they can be hard to shake. Because they provide an organizing framework, and are often imbued with emotional content, stories can overwrite and exaggerate our memories of an event.

Think of yourself as the night sky. What stars will you choose to connect into shapes? How will you choose to tell the story of yourself? There are so many ways to tell it, and all of them have some truth to them. Yet not all of them are equally useful. Remembering the good which came from the bad in your life, and emphasizing the elements of your life of which you are in control, are two sure ways to start to tell better stories about who you are. These kinds of stories trace a bright path for you towards fulfilling your potential and engaging in life.

Sources

Dingfelder, S. (2011, January). "Our stories, our selves". *Monitor on Psychology. American Psychological Association*. www.apa.org/monitor/2011/01/stories.aspx

Nicolaus, P. (2014, Sept 9). "Storytelling Q&A with Jonathan M. Adler". *Nicolaus Writing*. http://www.nicolauswriting.com/blog/storytelling-qa-with-jonathan-m-adler#.VW0BxFVViko

Zimmerman, R. (2012, January 3). "For mental health boost: take charge of your personal story". WBUR *Common Health: Reform and Reality*. www.commonhealth.wbur.org/2012/01/storytelling-for-mental-health-boost

N.a. (2016). 'The constellations'. International Astronomical Union. www.iau.org/public/themes/constellations/

APPLICATIONS:

RE-WRITE yourself!

APPLICATIONS AND SELF-DISCOVERY

The juncture between high school and your next step of training is an important one. You should know that, at least in my experience, there are many more scholarships available for you to apply for when you are first entering university than there will be in your next three or four years of schooling combined. If you would like to take the edge off of your student debt while learning about yourself at the same time, scholarship applications are your friend.

Before getting to the business of how to approach your applications, let's discuss a general system for determining which awards and bursaries to apply for. Ask your high school guidance counsellor, and find databases online (check a few) to compile a short list of scholarships that match your eligibility criteria. Be realistic about how much time you can devote to this endeavour, and if you find that there are too many contenders on your list, narrow it by estimating your probability of success. Look more carefully at the requirements for each application. Some might require a short essay, while others might need you to write pages and also secure multiple letters of reference. Some might require you to be a woman interested in engineering, while others might only be specific to a certain school. Note that if there are fewer requirements for an application, more people will likely submit one, so chances of success may be lower. Scholarship committees also tend to be quite particular about applicant characteristics. There is no point in applying if you do not fit their criteria. I had a third, unscientific criterion that I used when I was going through this process. I would not apply to a scholarship if it was less than $1000 dollars (about €720), because that number seemed significant to me, and I knew that I would try harder on the application if there was more at stake. Depending on the availability of awards in your region, that rule might not work for you, but if you still need to narrow down your options, find a rule that does fit your situation.

Once you have your realistic list of candidates, it is time to think about how you can enhance your experience during the process. After four years of filling out applications for various awards and scholarships, I finally realized that with a little bit of mental framing, these applications could be more than just a fundraising attempt. Many of the applications I wrote offered me the chance both to discover and to shape my identity. Knowing more about ourselves, our dreams, talents, experiences and skills is an absolute requirement for making good decisions. Applications allow us to tell different kinds of stories about ourselves. We can choose to repeat and emphasize the same story we've been telling about ourselves for years, or we can choose to take the raw data of our life experiences and spin them into a slightly different trajectory that would lead us to a wildly different future. Taking control of your story is empowering beyond belief.

In my case, for years, I had been telling a story about myself that emphasized my interest in complexity science. I framed my experiences at university as a quest to understand more about systems. Then, in the midst of a challenging internship program, I found myself questioning whether that story led where I really wanted to go. Suddenly, I saw a different line that fit the different data points of my life, but it told a very different story. Instead of being interested in complex systems, I was interested in the future of education. Both interpretations could reasonably come from the data, but by experimenting, I was able to find one that seemed to better fit my aspirations for the future.

Applications offer a structured way for you to experiment with your own story, until you find the one that seems to fit you the best (at least for the moment). This process of making and remaking your narrative reminds you that you are the author of your life. Who you imagine yourself to be is often the person that you will become, because your mindset will shape your choices.

Speaking of structure, it is important not to get so carried away with storytelling that you miss submission deadlines! I recommend keeping track of all due dates on your calendar or agenda, and working backward for each one so that you know when you should have your draft finished, or when you should request your letter of reference, or when you should have filled out the application form. Breaking large tasks like this into smaller pieces and scheduling them is a sure way to increase your chances of success (read our section on One Bite at a Time for more inspiration).

Whatever the outcome of your application, the knowledge you will gain about yourself and the sense of empowerment you will feel cannot be taken away from you. In my experience, however, the applications where I flexed my storytelling powers were the ones that tended to be the most successful. Authentic and earnest self-exploration makes you stand out from a crowd that is trying to conform to the mould of the ideal 'student'. One way or another, investing in self-discovery will pay off.

STRENGTH? WEAKNESS?

DEPENDS ON THE

ASSETS AND LIABILITIES: FINDING THE RIGHT CONTEXT

At some point along the journey to self-understanding, you will have to consider your strengths and weaknesses. What do you do really well? What do you do poorly? A common perspective is that these strengths and weaknesses are fixed, that, in every situation, you have the same talents helping you and gaps limiting you. But what if your ability to be empathic, which others usually tell you is one of your strengths, holds up your group from finishing your assignment before it is due. Everyone wants to work, but you know that people are stressed and in disagreement, so you think that you should all take time to talk and work through it. On the other hand, what if your task-oriented nature leaves your boyfriend cold. "I feel like I am just another thing to check off on your list!" he yells at you, and then walks away.

What counts as a strength or a weakness actually changes depending on the context. There are a few exceptions at the extreme ends (being very aggressive towards others, for example, though I suppose that if you were being mugged, it might end up being a strength), but if you list a few of the things you consider to be your weaknesses, I think that you might easily conceive of situations where they would be useful. Take me, for example. I tend to ignore what is happening around me when I am focused on a task. When I am at a library, this ability to focus is an extreme strength. When I am reading recreationally outside and my mother is trying to talk to me, this ability to focus makes her feel ignored. My ability to see the humour in most situations is great when I am at parties, but not so good at funerals.

Instead of trying to use the skills you think are your strengths and avoid the weaknesses, I encourage you to think about the various contexts you inhabit as you go through your life. What are your strengths and weaknesses in each of these contexts? If there is a lot of overlap, then you can continue with trying to stop some of your 'bad' behaviours. If not, decide which tradeoffs you can live with (and let's face it, we will always have to live with some tradeoffs!). If you survey your contexts and find that the elements of your character that you see as your strengths aren't actually helping you, consider finding different contexts to be in. Change is possible, but it takes time and effort, and it is often better to channel your existing characteristics in positive ways rather than trying to change them. People in your current situation might see your traits as liabilities, but try to find places where others will see them as assets. For example, if your tendency to want to stay on task and on schedule infuriates your laid-back band members, maybe you should join a robotics team instead.

Knowing that strengths and weaknesses are context-dependent is important if we want to know and accept our full selves. Everyone has a dark side, or at least dark patches, composed of the thoughts and traits that we suppress because we think that they are bad. Maybe you get very jealous, or maybe you are incredibly self-centred. Because we try to push these parts of us deep down, it can be hard to take a clear look at what these traits are. One exercise that I find to be incredibly powerful is one that I encountered in *Getting to Maybe*, a book about social innovation. To do this technique, you need to think of a person that you really and truly dislike, a person whose character you find unbearable. Describe them to yourself in detail, and write down the traits that you find especially hard to deal with. Then, take a look at those traits. Most often, these traits are ones that you suppress in yourself. They form your hidden dark side. In my case, the person I described was arrogant, opinionated, and unafraid to be mean. While in excess, these traits are undesirable, I realized that by suppressing all of their forms in myself, I was also losing out. I was trying to be too nice, too humble, and too quiet. I would not speak up when I thought something was amiss. I would allow others to be rude to me, and I would constantly second-guess myself. To be the strongest person I could be, I needed to incorporate some elements of the traits I had dismissed as being harmful.

Strengths and weaknesses are not nearly as clear-cut as you might think. Each context of your life requires you to re-label what is helpful and harmful. Before you try to eradicate what is bad from your character, think carefully about the good you might also be losing. Do not be afraid of your dark side. Seek to understand it, and embrace the light within it. What makes you strong also makes you weak. What makes you weak can also make you strong.

Sources

Quinn Patton, M., Westley, F., and Zimmerman, B. (2007). 'Getting to maybe: how the world is changed'. *Vintage Canada*: Toronto.

CHALLENGE YOUR ASSUMPTIONS

IDENTIFYING AND CHALLENGING YOUR ASSUMPTIONS

Do you ever think about the fact that you are moving through gas all the time? I am not talking about farts (though that happens sometimes!), I am just talking about the mixture of gases that make up our air; nitrogen, oxygen and argon. Because we can't see them, or really feel them, we tend to act like there is nothing around us. The fact remains that, all of the time, we are wading through these gases. Of course, when we have to hold our breaths, we remember that it is is not just 'nothing' that we have to inhale a few times a minute. Assumptions are kind of like that too. They are all around us, and without them we would find it very hard to live. It's simply too difficult and exhausting not to have opinions about ourselves and others. If we had to determine whether our parents had our best interests at heart each time we interacted with them, we would become anxious and distracted. Instead, we assume that our parents will support us, or that our school will still be open tomorrow, or that we will have to choose a career at some point in our lives. We make assumptions about so many different things, and most of them are harmless, if not helpful.

Still, there is a class of assumptions that need to be dealt with more carefully. These assumptions need to be carefully tested. They will be different for every person, but the main feature they share is that they are limiting. These assumptions keep you from attempting or achieving your goals. For example, you might decide that a career in dance is not for you because "No one makes money in the arts." Or, you might decide that you need to party a lot at university, rather than spending most of your time studying your area of interest because "That's what everyone does." On a broader level, there are larger limiting beliefs that come from your culture and upbringing. Your parents or family may have instilled in you the idea that making a hefty salary and living comfortably is the main point of your life. Or, you might believe that accumulating material possessions is more important than continuing your education. These limiting beliefs aren't always wrong (the lifestyle of a dancer can be quite difficult to manage, but there are many other careers in the arts that can offer you a more stable lifestyle if that is what you really want), but because so many of your important decisions will be shaped by them, it is very important to make sure that they are right for you.

The first step towards assessing a limiting assumption is sensing that it is there. I can sense that I am dealing with one of these beliefs when I am feeling very trapped and negative about a situation or decision. I can almost sense the belief as a set of iron bars that has dropped around me. Perhaps a phrase that your parents often say to you sets off the same kind of emotional reaction. Once you have sensed the belief, it is time to interrogate it.

If the assumption is data-based, *ie* "No one in the arts makes any money," use your internet sleuthing skills to test it. Even if an assumption is vague, like "Making money is the most important thing in life," you can turn it into a series of researchable propositions. You might examine how happiness and health correlate with wealth. Luckily, if a topic is important to you, it is likely important to others. You can do pretty well with putting your search question into Google and seeing whether it returns any newspaper or magazine articles as hits. If these articles are from reputable sources, and communicate recent research on your question, you are golden!

If you are curious, while rich people are on average happier than poor people, one component of happiness, the affective component (meaning how often you experience positive emotions), tops out after a salary of $75,000 American dollars (the study was conducted in the United States). I found that fact after a quick search of the phrase "how does wealth relate to happiness," on Google, and after checking the first few links to determine which articles had references to real scientific studies.

Some of the assumptions will not be checkable with data, but here are a few shortcuts to deal with some common ones. A limiting assumption about your own skills, such as "I am terrible at math" is a sign of a fixed mindset rather than a growth mindset (Please read our section on the Growth Mindset if you have any variety of these beliefs). You may have to work harder at math to build your skills, but it is not impossible, obviously. A limiting assumption about others, such as "People will judge me if I decide to become an electrician," is actually a sign of another limiting assumption "I have to make others around me happy with all of my choices." This belief is one that you will have to assess for yourself. I would encourage you to read our section about Caring what Others Think.

Assumptions can be tricky. Catch them when you sense they are blocking your way, and make sure they are there for a good reason. Otherwise, find new ones that are more empowering.

Sources

Blackman, A. (2014). 'Can money buy you happiness'. *The Wall Street Journal.* www.wsj.com/articles/can-money-buy-happiness-heres-what-science-has-to-say-1415569538

Be a Big Fish
in a Small Pond

BEING THE BIG FISH

Is it better to be a big fish in a small pond, or a small fish in a big pond? Many of you might say that it is always better to be challenged. Surely the big pond is the only way to go if you want to become excellent.

Interestingly, when we are talking about school choices, the answer is more complicated. In some cases, the smaller pond might be better. In his book, *David and Goliath*, investigative journalist Malcolm Gladwell featured the research of Herbert Marsh. Marsh examined what he called the 'academic self-concept', which can be more glibly referred to as whether a student thought himself or herself to be smart or stupid. Marsh studied two groups of students who had entered university with similar grade point averages. One group of these students went to universities where they were placed the lower rungs of intelligence, and the other group went to smaller schools, where they placed among the highest rungs of intelligence. Do you think that these students' academic self-concepts would differ? Marsh found that they did. The students in 'smarter' schools tended to think of themselves more poorly than the students in the 'dimmer' schools. Students in dimmer schools were more likely to graduate out of STEM (science, technology, engineering and mathematics) programs than were students in the more challenging schools.

As Gladwell points out, it wasn't as though the content of the courses could be that different. Chemistry is chemistry! What was at play was something Marsh called the "Big Fish Little Pond Effect." Students in the 'smarter' schools were constantly comparing themselves to their brighter classmates. They often felt inadequate. This negative self-concept made them psychologically weaker. They were more likely to give up when they faced challenges. Students in the 'dimmer' schools compared much more favourably to their peers. They felt on par with or ahead of their classmates, and this confidence gave them more motivation to stay the difficult course and complete their technical degrees.

Note that the students in the study had very similar 'absolute' measures of intelligence, assuming that grade point averages are some proxy to certain kinds of intelligence, of course! All that differed was their 'relative' intelligence. What does this finding mean for you? Who you compare yourself to is very important. Achieving Bs might be impressive to you if all of your friends are struggling along with C-minuses, but it will likely be a source of concern for you if you have befriended the star of your school's chemistry olympiad team. If the achievements of the person to whom you are comparing yourself seem within reach, you will probably feel motivated to close the gap. If the distance seems more like a chasm than a gap, you may become demoralized and give up.

Running with the big dogs is necessary for some goals, but not all of them. If achieving what you wish does not require attending a prestigious institution, and you have a sense that you would run the risk of being in the 'dim' section, your choice is probably worth a rethink. Still, the Big Fish Little Pond Effect is not a prescription for taking it easy. It merely makes the point that absolute measures of our skills matter less than relative measures. It is important to choose your learning and working environments carefully so that you are motivated to improve rather than completely demoralized. Aim for that appropriate level of challenge.

Sources

Seaton, M,, Marsh, H., and Craven, G. (2009). 'Big fish little pond effect: generalizability and moderation - two sides of the same coin'. *American Educational Research Journal*. http://aer.sagepub.com/content/47/2/390.abstract

Tomlinson, O. (2015). 'Malcolm Gladwell's mindblowing theory on why it's better to be a big fish in a small pond'. *Bit of News*. http://news.bitofnews.com/malcom-gladwells-mindblowing-theory-on-why-its-better-to-be-a-big-fish-in-a-small-pond/

COMPETE

— OR —

IGNORE?

THE IMPORTANCE OF DOING YOUR BEST

I had my fair share of academic rivals. To varying degrees, I competed with Lithuanian-Canadian, Ukrainian-Canadian and a pair of Polish-Canadian twins. These rivalries were mainly one-sided; they competed with me, but I did not carve up very much space in my head for them. In fact, once I got out of grade school, I had decided that the only person against whom I was competing was myself. I did not care what these boys of Eastern European heritage were doing. What concerned me more was whether I was giving something a good enough effort.

This change in perspective came from my family. I am so grateful to my mother for encouraging me to compare myself only to myself. All she wanted to know, when I brought home a result for some project, was "Did you do your best?". To her, that was all that mattered. Internalizing this idea helped me stay focused on my own improvement, rather than on what it might take to win. It has taken me a while to learn that sometimes, attempting to do your best in every domain is a recipe for disaster (read our chapter on Maximizing and Satisficing to share in what I discovered), but I am still glad that I never tied my sense of self-worth to another person. So long as I knew that I had maintained or improved my skills or knowledge, it did not matter what happened to other people.

I would like to think that I intuited the dangers of competition. It's too simplistic to say that the best person wins and the rest are losers. As we discuss in our section on randomness, each of us are dealt different hands. Winners might just be the ones whose hard work combines with talent, support and other environmental advantages. Many of you might be bristling after reading these lines. Perhaps you have had positive experiences with competition. Perhaps you like the adrenaline that courses into your veins when you realize you have a chance of winning. Your experiences are reflected by scientific literature. Competition isn't unequivocally bad. When researchers Murayama and Elliot examined 81 studies of competition and performance with almost 6000 total participants, they found no correlation. Competition did not significantly decrease performance, but it did not significantly increase it either. Murayama and Elliot argue that this lack of correlation is created by two effects cancelling each other out. Competitions increase performance by enhancing motivation, but they can also cause anxiety, which decreases performance. If competition allows you to focus on the task at hand, it helps. If it distracts you, it hurts. What kind of competitor are you? How does competition normally affect you? Only you can answer those questions.

The main issue with certain kinds of competitions is that they tend to emphasize winning rather than mastery. Take, for example, the story of Perdita Felicien. Coming into the 2004 Athens Olympics, she was considered the best female hurdler in the world. She had won the World Championships in 2003 and was considered a favourite for the gold medal. She progressed to the finals, but shockingly, tripped and fell over the first hurdle. I remember watching her fall on the televised broadcast of the Olympics that year. My heart broke at the unfairness. This mistake should not have defined her to the world, and yet it did. Even though she had run so many clean and fast races in practice, all that mattered was that she had lost.

Competitions are simplistic snapshots. They give us a point-in-time reading of how we measure up to others. I think that we would be better served by using them only to measure our own progress. We need to recognize that the winner does not take all. For more ideas on how to avoid the toxic aspects of competition, read our section about Blue Ocean Strategy.

Sources

Rivett, A. (2014). 'Pickering's perdita felicien recalls good, bad of her track-and-field career in upcoming autobiography'. *Durham Region News*. www.durhamregion.com/news-story/5326298-pickering-s-perdita-felicien-recalls-good-bad-of-her-track-and-field-career-in-upcoming-autobiograp/

Murayama, K, and Elliot, A. (2012). 'The competition-performance relation: a meta-analytic review and test of the opposing processes model of competition and performance'. *Psychological Bulletin*. https://www.psych.rochester.edu/people/elliot_andrew/assets/pdf/2012a_MurayamaElliot2012a.pdf

Richtel, M. (2008). 'The role of competitiveness in raising healthy children'. *The New York Times*. www.nytimes.com/2012/10/11/garden/the-role-of-competitiveness-in-raising-healthy-children.html?pagewanted=all&_r=0

Kohn, A. (1987). 'The case against competition.' *Working Mother*. www.alfiekohn.org/article/case-competition/?print=pdf

OTHERS AND THE OTHER

THE IMPORTANCE OF FEEDBACK: THE JOHARI WINDOW AND THE COMPETENCE MATRIX

When you look up at the stars, you can't help but notice that most of the sky is black. These tiny pinpoints of light are just sprinkled among the darkness. I think that this visual maps very well onto our own areas of knowledge and ignorance. There is so much that we do not know, and will never know. It is impossible to master all of the world's languages, or to know in great detail the history of the world. Yet, there are areas where the knowledge we don't have is well within our reach. A few more stars in a well-placed region of our night sky can do much to help orient us. The domain where I think we can beat back the darkness is self-knowledge.

Now, you're probably thinking, "Self-knowledge? Really? I probably spend more time thinking about myself than anything else. I'm probably the world's leading expert." Knowing more than other people does not make you an expert. If you do not have good answers to important questions such as "What will make me happy?", "What are my talents?", and "Where and how can I improve as a person?", you are not an expert. If you decide that you do need help, read on.

Thanks for staying along for the ride. The Johari window is your reward. It is a simple matrix, and it was drawn up in the 1950s by two psychologists, Joseph Luft and Harry Ingram. You probably noticed that I've drawn a version of it for the chapter image.

The Johari window helps to categorize different types of knowledge that you and others might have. If you see something in yourself, and others see it too, this forms part of your public self. Perhaps you think of yourself as friendly, and others would agree. If you know something is true about yourself, but others would not agree, that knowledge forms part of your private or hidden self. In my case, only very close friends know that I have a very dark and sometimes inappropriate sense of humour. If others see something in you that you do not see in yourself, this knowledge forms part of your so-called 'blind self'. If you feel terrified while giving a speech, but others see you as confident, this confidence is part of your blind self. It exists, but you were not aware of it. Finally, there is a very dark part of your sky called the unknown self. These are things about yourself that neither you nor others know. Perhaps if you've been lucky enough never to deal with a crisis, how you handle extreme pressure might be part of this unknown self. You or others might not know how to predict what you might do if you found out your house was on fire. Knowledge is the first step to any plan, and any decision to change, so knowing as much about yourself and your effect on others as is reasonable is a fantastic way to ensure that you make good choices.

I would encourage you to make your own Johari window and fill out the parts you can. What do you think others see in you? What do you think is hidden or unnoticed? Then, test those assumptions.

We talk a little about the importance of testing in our Depth of Processing section, but it bears mention here too. Testing is a way to get feedback on your understanding, skill level, and knowledge. Crucially, testing doesn't have to only happen in the classroom. So long as you are willing to endure the possibility of failure (a hint: start small), there are so many opportunities to test yourself and solicit feedback. If you are trying to understand whether you are a good friend or not, you can test this assumption with a simple question to a friend you trust. Still, don't ask a question if you aren't prepared for an honest answer. Something else that is important to remember is that you do not have to accept the word of a few people close to you as being gospel. Feel free to seek a second opinion if you don't think someone has judged you accurately, but be careful that you are not just trying to protect your ego.

Getting feedback on your actions helps to ensure that your blind self stays as empty as possible. But there is also another avenue to take if you want to increase your self-knowledge. Being adventurous, by exposing yourself to new situations, ideas and challenges, allows you to shed light on the murky unknown self. The excitement, fun, and sometimes danger of this suite of activities can help to balance the often tough work of hearing truth from others. For both approaches, the Johari window can be your compass as you chart a path towards self-understanding, adding stars of knowledge to your own night sky.

Sources

Lopez de Victoria, S. (2008). 'The johari window.' *World of Psychology.* Psych Central. www.psychcentral.com/blog/archives/2008/07/08/the-johari-window/

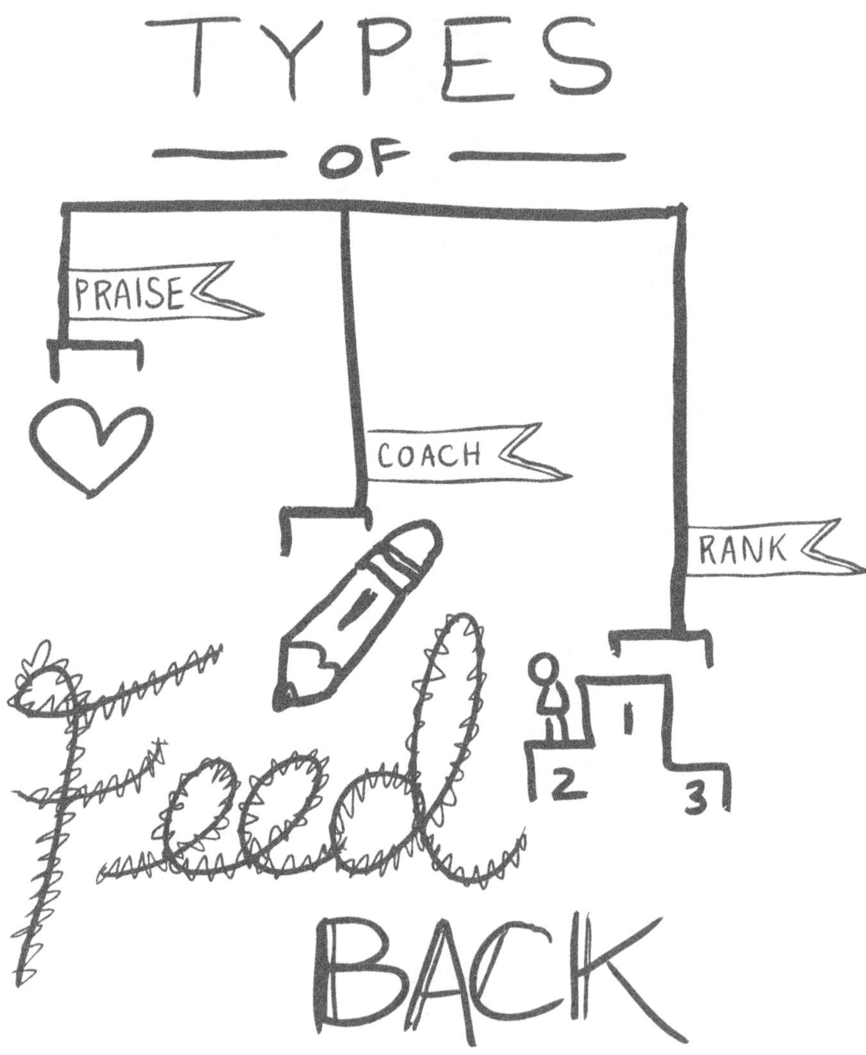
TYPES
OF
PRAISE
COACH
RANK
1
2
3
Feed
BACK

BEING ACCEPTED AND BEING INSTRUCTED: FEEDBACK PART II

We've already discussed why feedback is important, but what we haven't done is talk about why it can be so hard to hear and respond to. Sheila Heen and Douglas Stone, two lawyers who have spent 15 years mediating difficult conversations for non-profit and private organizations alike, understand the conundrum well. According to them, people seek feedback because they want to learn and grow, but this impulse competes with our desire to be accepted just as they are. Feedback that includes suggestions for improvement also carries with it an implicit judgment that the recipient is not good enough as she is.

Most people are conflict-averse, and many are not exceptionally self-aware, so we tend to be pretty terrible at giving feedback. We tend to choose vague words, and often might wait for much too long before saying anything. Perhaps because of this feedback-giving ineptitude, we are also pretty terrible at receiving feedback. We might respond too emotionally and derail the conversation, and we often focus more on finding reasons to reject the feedback than on trying to understand why and where it is coming from.

While we can't change other people (or at least we can't do so very easily), we do have power over how we respond to situations where we receive feedback. So much useful information is probably being squandered in your interactions with others, but that can change. An understanding of what types of feedback are commonly given, and the usual reasons why we dismiss feedback prematurely, can help you stay mentally present during these difficult conversations, and steer them towards a useful outcome.

There are many ways to categorize feedback, but Heen and Stone have devised three categories. The first is appreciative feedback. A "great job!" sticker your teacher affixes to your math assignment is an example of appreciative feedback, as it lets the recipient know that her efforts have been noticed and valued. The second type is coaching feedback, which focuses on how the person can improve her performance. When, sitting at the dinner table, my dad says that he could have cooked the chicken a little less, he is giving himself coaching feedback. He identified a problem (the chicken was too dry), and offered a suggestion for avoiding the problem (cook it less next time). The final type of feedback is evaluative, which tells you how you measure up to others. Seeing your name on a class ranking is a kind of evaluative feedback, as is hearing your mother say that your cookies are the best she has ever eaten.

Knowing that feedback can come in several different flavours is important, because what you think of as feedback is not necessarily how others would define it. Perhaps you are tired of the "good job!" stickers on your math assignments and instead want some coaching feedback so that you can improve your performance, so you get frustrated with your teacher. Or, maybe when your mother asks you what you think of her cooking, she is looking for appreciative feedback rather than evaluative feedback!

Across all types of feedback, people have a tendency to offer vague statements that are often unhelpful because they leave ample room for misinterpretation. Your teacher telling you that "You need to take this class more seriously," can be interpreted in many ways. You might think that she doesn't like the fact that you doodle in the margins of your notebook, but she might actually be trying to say that you need to attempt more challenge and bonus problems. This is a pretty innocuous example, but sometimes you can interpret vague feedback as a hurtful challenge to your character.

Coaching and evaluative feedback can both trigger emotional reactions. Even if it was not what the feedback-giver intended, you may feel as though you have been attacked. This emotional reaction might lead you to try to immediately discredit the feedback. Perhaps the observation was simply wrong. You might tell yourself, "I am not antisocial! I am just shy!". Or maybe the person who told you the information isn't someone you trust. "She doesn't know me! She just wants me to feel bad!" You might question the motive or qualifications of the person. Giving into these knee-jerk reactions can cause you to lash out at the feedback giver and lose your chance to make the conversation meaningful.

A better approach is to admit that you are feeling blindsided by using a phrase like, "What you're telling me goes against what I thought about myself, so I really want to make sure I understand you," which allows you to convey some of your emotion while still keeping the conversation going. Your goal is to get to the specifics of the feedback. Try to lift the blanket statement away from the observations that produced it. Offer your guesses as to the behaviours you think the other person might have issues with. Try, at all times, to make the other person feel safe in the conversation so that she does not respond defensively or emotionally either. Tell her that you value her perspective and want to understand what she is saying. There is no guarantee that her judgments are correct, but you can learn so much from understanding which behaviours or incidents led to the judgment being formed.

Should you always accept feedback? No. You may be too occupied with other obligations to make any changes, or you might have already decided on one aspect of your life that you want to improve. There is nothing wrong with listening and politely telling the person that while you understand what they are saying, at the moment you cannot address the behaviour because of extenuating circumstances. Be gracious, but firm. Feedback can be a wonderful source of clues for how to improve yourself, but you should be in control of it, not the other way around.

Sources

Heen, S., and Stone, D. (2014). 'Thanks for the feedback: the science and art of receiving feedback well'. *Viking Penguin*: New York.

(MOST) OTHERS

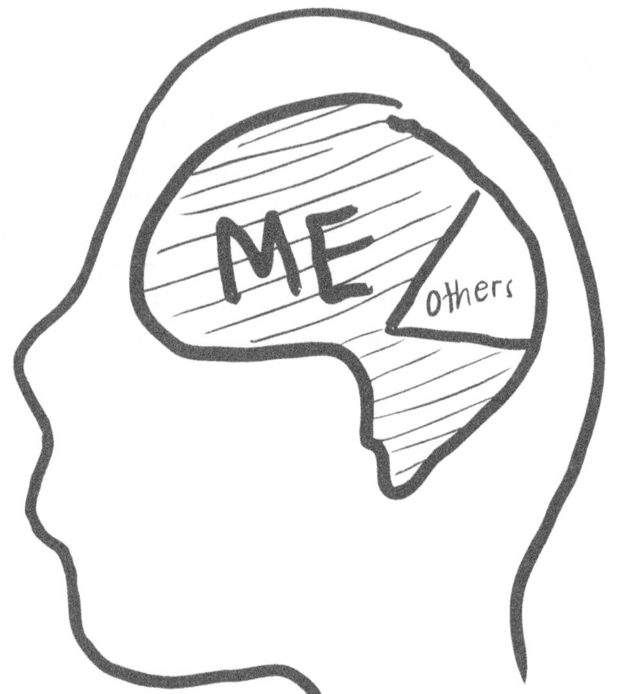

DON'T CARE ABOUT YOU MUCH!

CARING WHAT OTHERS THINK: A REALITY CHECK

Despite what motivational posters might tell you, developing a healthy relationship with the expectations of others is not quite as simple as deciding to "be yourself!". Many important questions need to be answered first. Why do we care so much about what others think? Is it helpful or harmful to do so? What can we do to change the sources of influence of our decisions? This section is all about helping you sift through myth and fact when it comes to the opinions of other people.

What are some of the facts? Firstly, our desire for approval is wired in at the neurological level. Brain research from the University College of London has shown that when people are informed that their opinions align with those of experts, they experience increased activity in the area of their brains associated with reward. The amount of increase in this 'reward area' is correlated to how easily the test subject is influenced by other people.

Secondly, concern for others' opinions makes sense on an evolutionary level as well. Human beings evolved for life on the savannah. They lived in 40-person tribal groups, and because of all the dangers that abounded, being accepted by other members of the tribal group was necessary for survival. Tim Urban of the science and social psychology blog *Wait But Why* argues that this evolutionary milieu resulted in us developing an internal, self-criticizing mammoth. Many of the mammoth's assumptions – that everyone around us deeply cares about what we do, and that we have to please everyone – makes sense for the 40-person tribal environment. As you might have observed, the human race is no longer operating in a 40-person tribal environment. Society and culture have developed at warp speed. The assumptions of the self-criticizing mammoth are no longer appropriate for your lives, in which there are vastly more than 40 people, and by which pleasing all of them is impossible.

Moreover, with the pace of modern life, it is highly doubtful that many of your friends and acquaintances spend large portions of their time concerned with your decisions. Just think of how little time you spend considering and judging the choices of your own friends.

Further research into our self-perception by Dr. Nicholas Epley at the University of Chicago showed that people do have some insight into what others think of them. We know, generally, whether others think we are intelligent, hard-working, funny, or attractive. We are terrible, however, at predicting what any one person thinks of us. Our insight only works at an aggregate level. One implication from this study is that if you are obsessing over how much someone dislikes you, especially if this assumption is based on shoddy evidence, you are likely wrong.

What do all of these facts mean for you? Firstly, recognize that conforming to others' expectations feels good, but know that it is because of how your brain is wired. It may feel great in the short-term, but understand that a pattern of choices meant only to please others will lead you to feel trapped and resentful in the long term. Remember your future self when you are making choices, not just the people around you at the moment. Secondly, when you experience anxiety about your choices, ask yourself whether it is the ancient mammoth talking, and whether its fears are truly relevant for the current day. Lastly, if you have a theory about how someone is judging you, test it. Do not trust your intuition.

If your actions aren't being driven by a fear of what others will think, what should be driving them? Two fantastic candidates are your own self-understanding and your strategic assessment of your circumstances. Make choices that work for your goals.

Sources

Urban, T. (2014) 'Taming the mammoth: why you should stop caring about what other people think.' www.waitbutwhy.com/2014/06/taming-mammoth-let-peoples-opinions-run-life.html

Lawes, P. '10 things to remember if you care too much about what others think'. www.lifehack.org/articles/communication/10-things-remember-you-care-too-much-about-what-others-think.html?bd=2015527

Epley, N. (2014). 'Misunderstanding what others think, feel, believe, and want'. *Capital Ideas.* www.chicagobooth.edu/capideas/magazine/spring-2014/misunderstanding-what-others-think-believe-feel-and-want

Callaghan, T. (2010).'The brain science behind why we care what others think.' *TIME.* www.healthland.time.com/2010/06/17/the-brain-science-behind-why-we-care-what-others-think/

FIND AN HONEST CHEERLEADER

FIND AN HONEST CHEERLEADER

My oldest friend is what you'd call a straight-shooter, which is funny because for the longest time, her job was to stop pucks (she's a hockey goalie). We met when we were in kindergarten, and despite how differently we have turned out, we somehow remained pretty friendly until the end of university, when geography drove us apart. My other friends did not fully understand why we still hung out with each other, and when they asked me, all I could say was, "She's not afraid of me."

Even at my angriest, I am not a very scary person, but what I meant by that comment was that this friend wasn't trying to make me like her. If she thought something I was doing was stupid, she would tell me (most often, she would laugh at me), even if it might cause conflict between us. Over the years, I grew more and more concerned with pleasing others through my comments and behaviour, so when she would be extremely direct with me, I would be floored. I could not imagine being as honest with anyone as she was being with me.

Being friends with her has helped me realize something important. It is so easy to be nice to those around you. You can avoid conflict pretty much forever using this technique, but all that you are doing is showing how little you care about your so-called friends. If your friends and mentors do not care enough about you to want you to improve, that is a bad sign. They are not the kind of people you want in your corner.

The folk tale about the emperor and his new clothes makes this point in a colourful way. None of the townspeople wish to tell the emperor that his new clothes don't exist, because they are afraid of what he might do to them. But, as a result, he parades around naked, embarrassing himself. You want people who will tell you when your clothing is see-through, and when you are being rude. Being honest when it counts shows your integrity. It took me too long to realize that being nice was really a way to be hurtful to people I thought I cared about. Now I understand that I can and should be giving them the honest, yet kind responses I have received in the past.

Of course, lying, whether directly or by omission, is a part of our culture for a reason. Not every scenario is worth the negative emotions and conflict that honesty can bring. Moreover, *how* you go about talking to a person about a sensitive topic is as important as what you say. At all costs, you want to avoid making them feel unsafe. Clarify your intentions and goals at the beginning of a conversation. Speak to them as someone who cares about them, and whose goal is to help them live a better life. If you are on the receiving end of one of these critical observations, try to be charitable when you are guessing the intention of the other person.

For example, I was part of an eight-month leadership development program. It was quite a challenging environment. All of the 25 participants were given total freedom to decide how to spend their time. With so much choice, I became stuck in an optimizing frame of mind, and kept second-guessing my commitments (read more about the dangers of optimizing in our section on that). For one of the first times in my life, I was not following through on promises I had made. One of the managers of the program approached me and asked if we could take a walk together. When I agreed, we set out for a park. He told me how much he respected me, and said that this respect led him to want to give me feedback about my lack of 'grit' (the ability to push through things and finish). There were several points at which I felt uncomfortable during the conversation, but overall, I was very grateful that he had put his own needs second to mine and approached me. He did not have to do this; he could have simply avoided collaborating with me until the end of the program. But, by delivering difficult feedback in a kind and direct way, he won my trust forever. He also motivated me to correct the bad habits I had picked up when it came to finishing (read our section on the Dark Side of Quitting).

It is not enough to be merely honest; people will hate you, but being nice is not a long-term solution for anyone. What we should aim for is to be honest cheerleaders, people who genuinely want others to succeed, and who are willing to provide honest feedback in an open and kind manner when it counts.

MIND HACKS

FEELING FOLLOWS ACTION

"I don't feel like it."

This realization used to stop me in my tracks. Waiting for motivation that never came, I kept postponing the long walk in the park to see the fall leaves, or starting to write the story of my life. Sometimes, faced with an assignment so complex it seemed menacing, I felt the will to engage with it leave my body. The flightiness of my wants infuriated me. I was letting my feelings control me, at the expense of being able to do some of the things I really cared about. I hated it.

In some instances, I developed workarounds. I would start reading through the complex assignments just to see whether they were really as terrible as I had feared. I would soon notice, to my surprise, that once I had read the instructions over for a few minutes, I suddenly felt like engaging with the material.

Then, I had a life-changing realization; sometimes, feeling follows action. You don't feel like drawing but you start drawing and all of a sudden you begin to commit to the activity. Once you have dug your wheels into the dirt and started moving, your momentum carries you.

Waiting for the perfect time might mean waiting forever. Unless the anti-death crusaders prevail, none of us has that long. I felt liberated when I realized that feelings were pieces of information, not dictates. They can (and should) influence our actions, but our actions can and should definitely influence them.

Now, if you try a task and after a while the feeling remains, that feeling is probably worth listening to. There is a difference between not feeling like doing something, despite having the mental energy to do so, and not being capable of doing something because you are exhausted. Often, however, we just need a bit of a boost to get started, just like a car that has stalled in a grocery store parking lot. Try to power through, and you may surprise yourself!

REJECT FUNCTIONAL FIXEDNESS

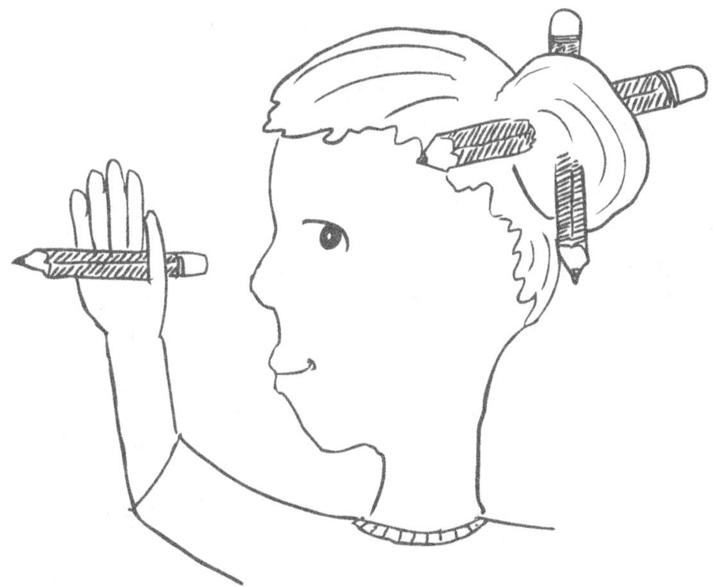

ONE THING

FUNCTIONAL FIXEDNESS

What differentiates a ceramic flower vase from a ceramic cup? Both can hold water. Both are solid and hollow. Both are fragile. Some flower vases look very much like large ceramic cups. Yet, if you saw someone drinking from something you had been told was a ceramic vase, you would think they were a little odd.

Functional fixedness is what happens when we believe that the label we give to an object completely defines it. A candle can only be burnt. It cannot be used as a doorstop or a crayon, because, after all, it's a candle! Its wick cannot be used to tie a bow because, as we all know, a wick should only get burned. Functional fixedness stops us from seeing the many other roles that household objects might be able to play in our lives. Functional fixedness does not just extend to household objects, however. We can be similarly unimaginative when we think about more consequential things. We might think of our mother only as our nurturer, and overlook the fact that she has a depth of experience in chemistry that we might be able to use to help us with our small business idea. We might see school as a place where we study, as opposed to a place where we can discover more about ourselves. We might think that our end of term projects can and should only exist within the walls of our school.

But what's stopping you from using your end-of-term project as a way to meet ten people who are pursuing careers you find interesting? Who is to say that a story you write for a creative composition class can't be submitted to your library's youth magazine. Why can't your explanation of a math problem be uploaded on Youtube so that it might help other students?

These are all examples of what I call 'objective stacking', when you move past functional fixedness to discover multiple uses for an activity or project. The simple logic of objective stacking is that you will have to do the work no matter what, so why not make it really count? When you are faced with a substantial task, refuse to so easily accept that you cannot get more bang for your effort.

Some of these examples involve a small amount of additional work, but this effort should not be significant. You should be spending less time than if you did the projects separately. If not, consider whether the additional activity is worth your time (the answer might still be yes!). Sometimes having externally-imposed responsibilities or deadlines can allow you to prioritize something you may have originally postponed. Try to make the major forces of your life work for you rather than against you. (See our section on Surfing and Randomness for more information).

Objective stacking is not always possible. Sometimes, you won't have the skills necessary to pull it off, or, even if you do, you might decide that your time is better spent elsewhere. Still, thinking through non-obvious ways to use your work to further your goals is a terrific habit to develop. Planning for objective stacking can occur systematically, at the beginning of a project, or organically, as opportunities present themselves. See our section on Scanning for more advice on how to coax opportunities your way.

Sources

Cherry, K. (2015) 'Functional fixedness'. *About Psychology.* www.psychology.about.com/od/problemsolving/f/functional-fixedness.htm

SYSTEM ONE
+
SYSTEM TWO
= A POWERFUL
TEAM

SYSTEM 1 AND SYSTEM 2

I looked across the table and decided that the moment was right. I looked her in the eye and asked, "Do you ever feel like you have two people inside of you?"

"Are you pregnant?" responded my friend, laughing.

"No, I mean, two versions of yourself" I told her. "One version that thinks, and another that is more like an animal?"

"Like Dr. Jekyll and Mr. Hyde?" She asked.

"Minus the evil murdering aspect" I replied, and then decided never to bring it up again.

Not being able to talk about it with anyone made my whole experience even more strange. Perhaps you can relate, but I do feel as though I have two modes of being. One Brianna is the kind of person who lays out her gym clothes the night before and packs a healthy lunch. The other Brianna lurches out of bed and mindlessly makes her way to work. One Brianna is very thoughtful with what she says. The other Brianna is clumsy and impulsive. Sometimes, the more put-together Brianna develops plans to trick the other Brianna into making good choices. She can out-think her counterpart. She knows that if the gym schedule is not printed and attached to Brianna's day planner, the second Brianna will not go. It seems as though one Brianna is the Brianna from the past, always planning and acting for the future, and the other is Brianna in the present, always reacting.

I probably would have never mentioned this fact to anyone if I had not learned about System 1 and System 2. Psychologist Daniel Kahneman won a Nobel Prize for differentiating between these two modes of thinking in the brain. System 1 is fast, intuitive, and sometimes emotional. System 2 is slower, logical, and analytical.

System 2 is at work when I decide that it would be a good idea to pack my lunch before I go to bed. System 1 is at play when I decide to go to the gym after seeing the schedule in my bag (though it was System 2 that helped me decide to put it there in the first place). Neither one is necessarily 'better' than the other. System 2 is more deliberate and systematic than System 1, but if we used it all the time we would never be able to move through the countless decisions that make up our days, many of which aren't necessarily logical in nature (what to wear, or what to think about on our walk to school). System 1 is very efficient, but it is also very strong. It is so quick that it can bypass System 2, which is what happens when you decide to eat potato chips because they are on a table in front of you, even though you know you should not eat them.

So, as it turns out, we all do have two people inside of us. But what does this knowledge mean for you? This knowledge becomes power when we consider habits, which are at the interface of System 1 and System 2. A habit is something triggered by System 1; we do it without thinking. And yet, how something becomes a habit is in the domain of System 2. Using System 2, we can program better habits into our brain. Telling you that this is possible and that you should do it is not the same as telling you it is easy. Building better habits means that you have to accept and understand both of your mental systems. Our culture has a habit of prizing reason over emotion, and you might feel ashamed of your System 1, but you should not. Without System 1, you would not survive. System 1 is an ally you need to work with to achieve a life that will make everyone in your head happy. Using System 2, you can get into the 'head' of System 1 and design barriers and triggers to push you away from certain activities and towards other ones.

Our next sections will dive into tactics for understanding, building and destroying habits. What is important for now is that you become comfortable with and appreciative of the different systems in your head.

Sources

Bhalla, J. (2014). 'Kahneman's mind-clarifying strangers: system 1 & system 2'. *Errors we Live By*. BigThink. www.bigthink.com/errors-we-live-by/kahnemans-mind-clarifying-biases

Ciotti, G. '5 scientific ways to build habits that stick'. *99u*. www.99u.com/articles/17123/5-scientific-ways-to-build-habits-that-stick

WILLPOWER DEPLETES

USE IT WISELY

ON HABITS: PART I

Doing the right thing will always be a challenge, but there's no reason to make it any harder than it needs to be. In fact, you have every reason to make doing the hard thing as easy as possible. Have no clue what I mean? Read on!

You can't run forever: you'd collapse, completely out of energy. We have to eat and sleep to replenish our energy. Willpower is like that too. It runs out if you use it too much, and varies in step with our energy levels. When you are tired or stressed, you have less willpower than when you are well-rested and calm. Low willpower leads you to make choices that might make sense in the short term (*eg* watching that episode of the meaningless reality TV show your friends have been talking about) but come back to haunt you in the long term (*eg* staying up until 3am working on this assignment because you were watching meaningless TV for hours in the early evening).

When you have low willpower, even the tiniest of barriers (*eg* your workout clothes being in the hard to reach part of the closet) will be insurmountable. What does this mean for you? First, you should try to keep your willpower high. Sleep well, eat well (eating smaller meals, drinking adequate water, and healthy snacking throughout the day), cultivate inner calm (our chapter on Mindfulness will be a help for that), and remove tolerations from your life. What are 'tolerations'? They are anything that bothers you and saps your energy, but not enough to merit the energy it takes to fix them. It could be something like not having a garbage can in your room (so you have to keep getting up to throw things out), or anything that causes you moments of unhappiness on a regular basis. They might not seem worth tackling individually, but if you identify several of them (keeping a list for a week might help you think of them), removing them in an afternoon can be energizing in the short term and help protect your willpower in the long run.

As we all know, good intentions don't always lead to the hoped-for outcomes. You might be tired, hungry, and stressed. It happens to all of us. That's why it's important to have a second line of defense. You can often see the times when you're stretched thin coming from a few kilometres away. You can prepare. You need to do all that you can to make the right course of action the easiest thing for you to do. Want a small example? Knowing you will be less alert and less efficient in the morning (when hunger is the main thing on your mind) might lead you to make some of your decisions the night before (What will I eat for lunch? What will I wear? What do I need to bring to school?) so you can save your willpower for more important choices. Knowing that you might need to remove all barriers to working out in the morning might lead you to leave your gym clothes and running shoes on the chair next to your bed.

Make your default choice the awesome one. If you don't want to be distracted by the internet when you're doing your homework (assuming you don't need the internet for your homework), study in a place that doesn't have wifi, or leave your computer in another room. If you want to eat healthier, don't buy junk food. Try to intervene further upstream to head off distractions and barriers.

Still, there will be times when, despite all your efforts, you fail. You may suddenly find your shirt covered in potato chip crumbs and your Latin textbook unopened. In these moments, it is important to forgive yourself, and to seek to understand what is happening. Is there anything you can do to keep yourself focused? Do you need to revisit your motivations for doing your courses?

Be warned as well that we're only talking about removing possible distractions from certain parts of your life. If you start to be fundamentally bored by your existence, this is not a good sign. Willpower is optimized when you are healthy and challenged. The point of being able to make good choices is not so that you can be more and more productive, or do more and more of what other people want you to do. It's actually about finding ways to do what is required of you while still keeping your internal spark alive. So, if you find that you finish an assignment earlier because of good choices, reward yourself. Don't rush to fill all of your gained time with more of whatever you consider work (unless you absolutely have to). Take care of yourself, because you are worth it.

Sources

Sethi, R. (2009). 'Barriers are your enemy'. *IWT Blog*. www.iwillteachyoutoberich.com/blog/barriers-are-your-enemy/

Aujia, D. (2014). 'Remove all tolerations'. www.50waystogetajob.com/mission/remove-all-tolerations

UNDERSTAND

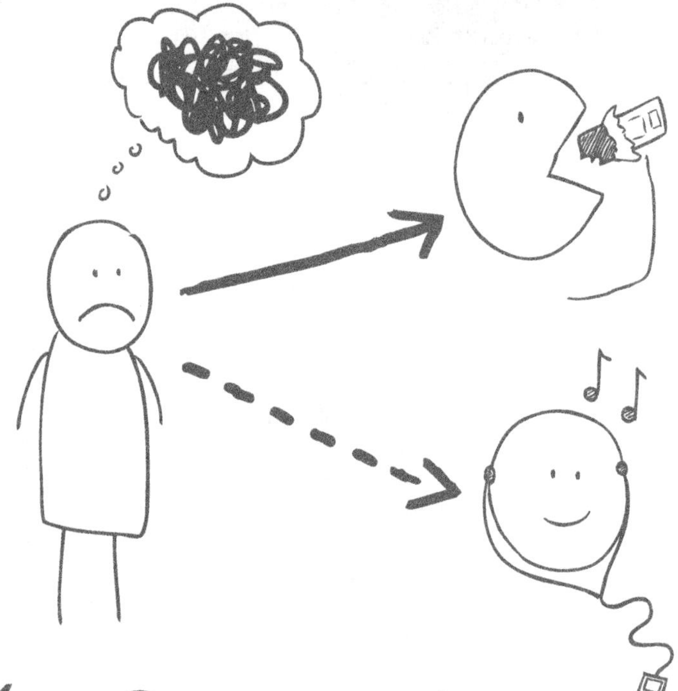

YOUR OWN BAD HABITS TO SWAP IN BETTER ONES

HABIT DESTRUCTION? HABIT REPLACEMENT!

Do you have any bad habits? Whether your grab-bag of negative behaviours includes procrastination, emotional eating, celebrity gossip-checking, picking your nose, or biting your nails, I would bet the proverbial family farm that it is not empty! Every day, chances are, you find yourself engaging in a behaviour that you will later regret. Why do we have such a hard time simply stopping negative behaviours?

One answer is that we are too shallow-sighted. When we try to change our patterns, we only focus on the behaviour itself. We decide that it is bad, and that we are bad people for continuing to do it. We make ourselves feel guilty, and decide that it is just because of our lack of willpower or moral fibre that we are not being better people. In face of this self-guilting tactic, however, the bad behaviour refuses to leave us. All that we succeed in doing is making ourselves feel defeated.

I think that the key to cracking the problem of bad habits is to flip our perspectives about them. Instead of criticizing ourselves for being weak people, I think we should ask ourselves what makes these bad habits 'good' for us? What need are they serving? How do they help us? I will use my own activities as an example. For years, I had been getting angry at myself for reading celebrity news and gossip, and for years, this anger had gotten me nowhere. Then, while researching for this book, I read an article by Leo Babuta, a blogger who has popularized zen thinking. He argues that the real reason we continue bad habits is that they allow us to deal with feelings of boredom and stress. We don't know how to cope without them. A bad habit is something we use to protect and comfort ourselves.

This idea led me to look at my own gossip-reading habit with much more compassion. I noticed, without judgment, that I tended to look for articles when I was feeling lonely, or bored. Believing that I was a terrible person for reading gossip made me feel stuck, but when I understood where the habit was coming from, I felt more free. I realized that the key to dealing with these behaviours was to figure out what deeper need was triggering me, and to then take steps to enrich my life in other ways to meet this need.

In my case, I decided to take an online drawing class, a subject about which I am genuinely passionate. Once I started drawing, I noticed that I spent less and less time on the gossip websites. I felt much better about myself. Do I still venture onto these websites? Yes, occasionally, but I take each of these events as information rather than an indictment of my character.

Now that we know a general approach for breaking bad habits, what are some real tactics I can pass on to you? I think the most useful thing I can tell you is that a habit has a few sub-components. Charles Duhigg, author of a book on habits, calls these the cue, routine, and reward. The cue is what triggers the activity. Think of the bell ring that caused Pavlov's dogs to drool. The trigger for your emotional eating might be feeling a certain kind of sadness. Once the cue has triggered you, then you start the routine. Maybe you reach for the bag of chips in your cupboard, or maybe you decide to watch a movie on your laptop. Carrying out this routine leads to some kind of reward. The sad feelings lift, and you feel less bored. This positive reinforcement encourages your brain to remember this set of activities for the future.

Your habit can be disrupted and re-routed by paying special attention to all three of these components. If you can remove your triggers, you will remove the habit. My choice to start taking a drawing class dealt with my triggering feelings of boredom. If you can't remove the triggers, you can try to disrupt the routine of the habit. If you don't buy potato chips, when you try to reach for them, they won't be there, and you likely won't marshall the energy to go and get some from the store. Or, if you cut some fresh carrots and celery at the beginning of the week and put them in the fridge for snacking, you might make a bee-line for them instead of eating nothing. This is a situation that requires ample use of System 2. Try to create micro-barriers around the bad habit's routine to make it harder to complete. For example, when you are going to bed, put your laptop in another room to discourage you from staying up late watching junk TV. Even the reward component of the habit can be used to your advantage. If you successfully divert your behaviour to a healthier habit, celebrate mentally.

Bad habits are misunderstood giants. They can crush us unless we know their secret: if we deal with them with compassion and intelligence, they can point us towards areas of our life that are ripe for enrichment.

Sources

Burkeman, O. (2009). 'This column will change your life: How Long Does it Really Take to Change a Habit?'. *The Guardian*. www.theguardian.com/lifeandstyle/2009/oct/10/change-your-life-habit-28-day-rule

Babuta, L. (2012). 'The habits that crush us'. www.zenhabits.net/crush/

Gross, T. (2012). 'Habits: how they form and how to break them'. *Fresh Air*. National Public Radio. www.npr.org/2012/03/05/147192599/habits-how-they-form-and-how-to-break-them

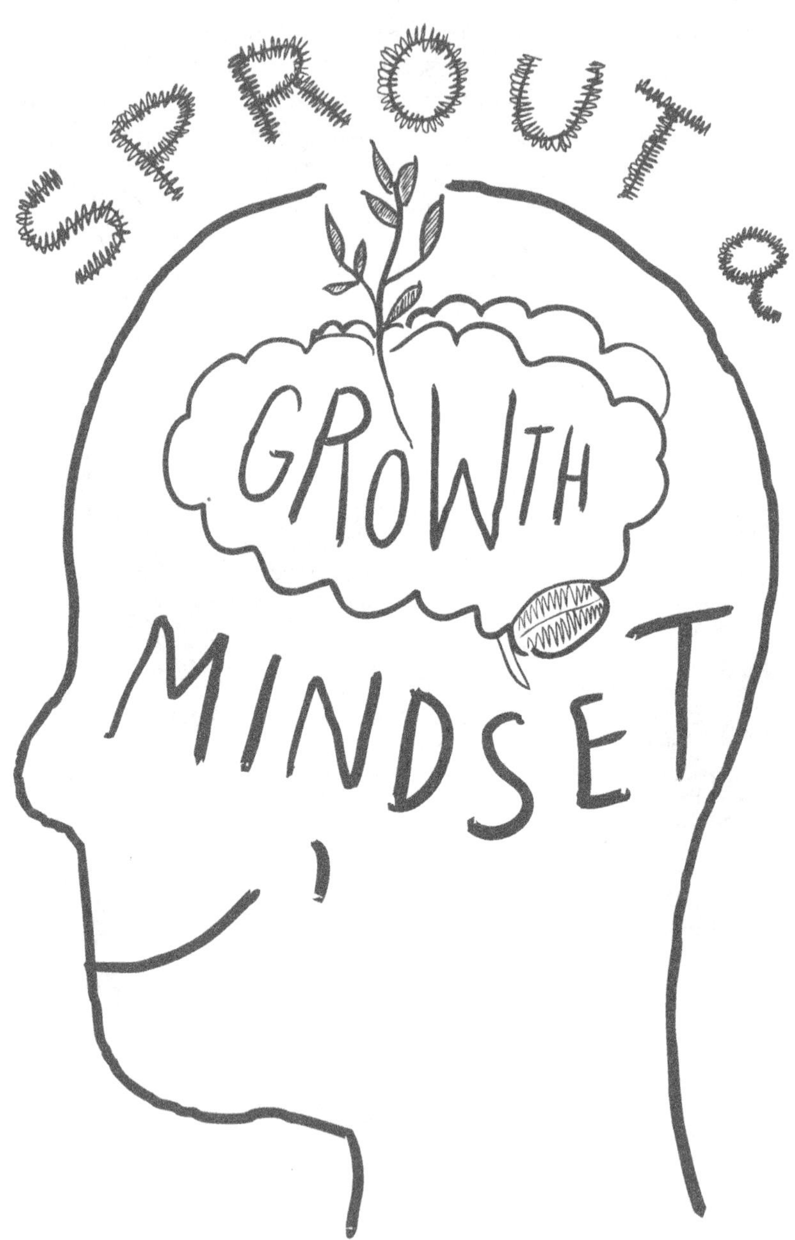
SPROUTe
GROWTH
MINDSET

GROWING A GROWTH MINDSET

What is your opinion of hard work? Do you think that it is a sign of stupidity? You probably don't, but I used to, and I haven't completely changed my opinion. My changing relationship with hard work illustrates some of the hidden costs of success. Throughout elementary and high school, I was praised for my intelligence. I worked diligently, but I now understand that I was focusing on my performance more than my learning. I used the same system for studying in grade six as I used in my last year of high school. I refused to experiment with ones that could have been more efficient. Why? I was unwilling to accept the momentary drop in performance that might result from any changes, despite the fact that in the long run, I would probably be better off. I saw my intelligence as something innate, rather than something I could constantly develop.

I now know that I had the classic symptoms of a fixed mindset. Stanford psychologist Carol Dweck has spent decades carefully investigating this topic. People with a fixed mindset tend to attribute their success to qualities they were born with and did not have to work for. People who attribute their success to hard work, and believe that they can develop new abilities fall into a different category, called the growth mindset. Dweck has shown that in the long term, people with the growth mindset end up being more successful. They are able to deal with challenging situations without having their self-confidence deflate, because they believe that even if they are not able to solve a problem now, with effort they will be able to solve it in the future. People with a fixed mindset accept the initial failure and decide that they have reached the limits of their ability. They give up.

The difference between a fixed mindset and a growth mindset is that the first focuses on performance, while the second focuses on learning and development. The first understands abilities as stone blocks of a certain height, while the second sees them as plants that can be watered. The first is concerned with the current y-coordinate, while the second is concerned with the slope of the line (Is it positive? Am I improving?).

Learning about the growth mindset was a revelation for me, but I haven't totally embraced the idea that hard work is the answer to all my problems. My qualm about 'hard work' being the answer to surmounting tough obstacles is that it is not always a strategic response. This advice seems to imply that if you just do more of what you were doing before, you will succeed. Of course, there are only a few cases for which this approach will work (It would be appropriate when you are guessing and checking a solution to a simple equation in mathematics, I suppose!). Perhaps we should be more charitable about this suggestion. 'Hard work' could also mean taking the time to think carefully about what is not working. It could mean re-learning certain parts of a concept you thought you had mastered. It could be anything that does not involve you giving up.

Still, there are clearly differences in the natural aptitudes of people, and is it really worth additional effort to try to cultivate a skill that you are not naturally gifted in, if this comes at the cost of neglecting an area where you have a foundation of talent? Perhaps not, but mastering any area of talent will involve being faced with challenges and activities that cause you to stretch beyond what you thought was possible. Dweck's findings do not claim that hard work is the answer to any obstacle, but they do tell us that people who try to persevere in the face of these obstacles have a greater chance of developing and learning than people who give up easily.

So, how can you cultivate a growth mindset? Reality-checking your assumptions about whether people really care what you do is a great first step, especially if you feel pressure to perform rather than learn (See our section on Caring what Others Think for more details). Finding arenas where it is safe to fail may help you become comfortable with brushing up against your limits and then learning how to push past them (See our section on Safe Fails). Understanding the plasticity of your own brain can give you evidence-based ammunition to fight a war with your deep-set assumptions (We have a section on that too! It's called Identifying and Challenging your Assumptions).

Sources

Krakovsky, M. (2007). 'The effort effect.' *Stanford Alumni Magazine*. https://alumni.stanford.edu/get/page/magazine/article/?article_id=32124

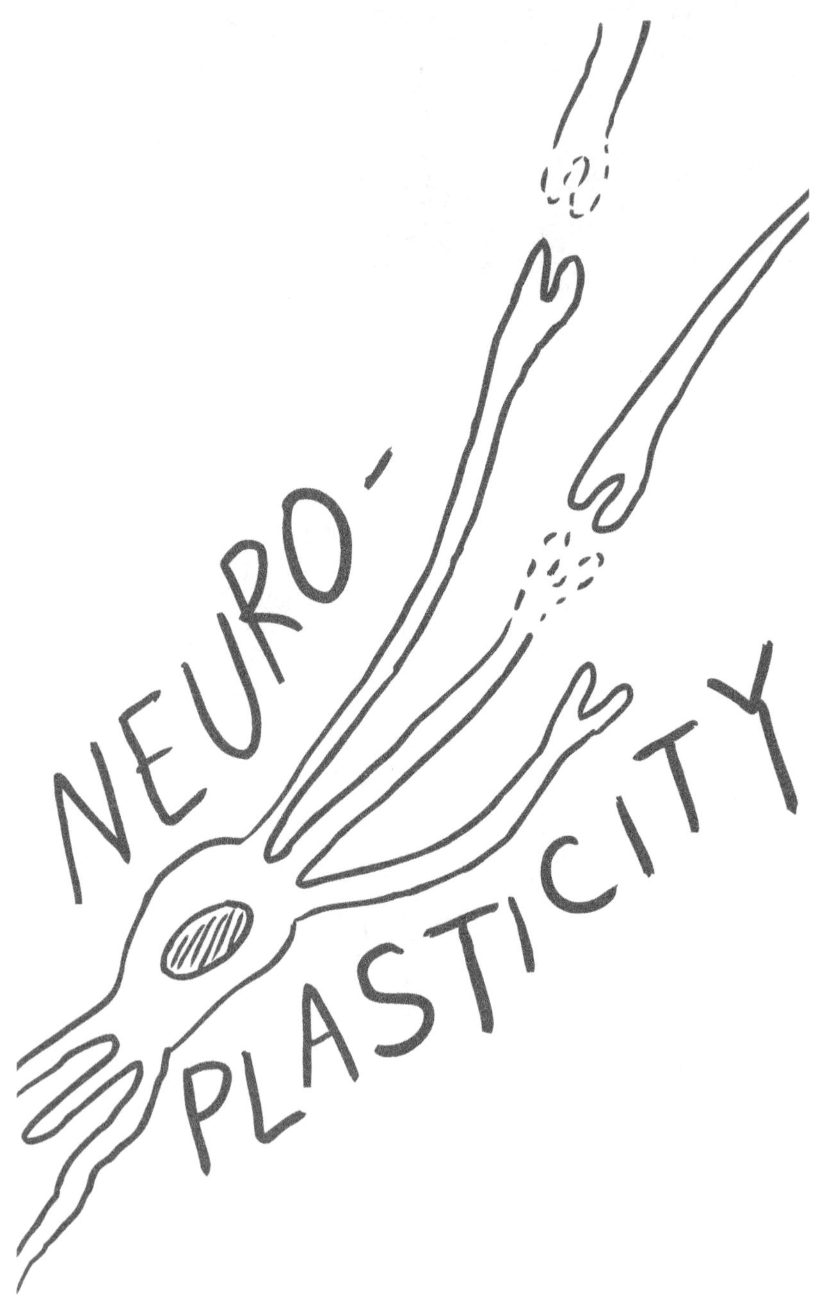
NEURO-
PLASTICITY

NEUROPLASTICITY: A DOUBLE-EDGED SWORD

It's not often that I can summarize a difficult concept in a few pithy little sentences, but this one is an exception. Neurons that fire together, wire together. Neurons that fire apart, wire apart. It is important to know how your brain works, because if you want to change it you have to know the rules. By now you probably know that our brains can and do change (how else do we manage to store all the information and skills we learn as we grow older?), but I think that having a basic understanding of the mechanics will help you make sense of why it can be so easy to get stuck in patterns of thought and action, and so very hard to change.

Your brain is made of cells, and many of those cells are neurons. Neurons connect to each other at junctions called synapses. We have Canadian neuroscientist Donald Hebb to thank for coming up with accurate and easy to remember phrases about how the brain changes. When one neuron is activated and 'fires' an electric signal, it travels down the neuron until it reaches the synapse, which acts as a gateway to activating another neuron. You will likely cover these concepts in your biology class in much more detail, but most synapses are chemical in nature. The electric signal must be converted into a chemical signal and back before it can continue to travel along the next neuron (this, of course, ignores the fact that multiple neurons can synapse to the same single neuron, and that some synapses can actually make it harder for the neuron to which they are connected to be activated). When a connection between two neurons is repeatedly triggered (*ie*, they 'fire' together), certain chemicals are released that make the synapse more efficient. The signal is more easily transferred from one neuron to the next, and for this reason, we might say that they 'wire' together. Of course, this principle is at play with complex interactions between many different neurons and synapses. When we learn how to ride a bicycle, neurons that fire together are wiring together, so that the behaviour becomes unconscious and requires much less mental effort or concentration. Patterns of thought behave like this as well. The more you think about something, the more you tend to think about it.

The converse of this rule is that second phrase. Your brain, just like any other part of your body, has to contend with finite resources. It can't justify wasting resources on areas of the brain that aren't very active. Just as activity between neurons can cause changes that lead to connections strengthening, lack of activity can cause connections to get much weaker, or even die away.

In short, our experiences and thoughts change our brains. Our brains are malleable, kind of like rubber, hence the term neuroplasticity.

You might think that the neurons wiring together is always good, while connections fading away is always bad, but if you have ever been gripped by a bad habit, you have experienced the dark side of neurons wiring together. If you've ever found that unpleasant memories become less clear as time passes and you are exposed to new events, the 'good' kind of firing apart has been at work for you.

Beyond the rhyming sentences, the most important thing for you to understand about how your brain changes is the fact that changes snowball. It gets easier and easier to make certain choices or have certain thoughts the more that you do them, and as a result it is harder and harder to divert from your course of action. Neuroplasticity helps you understand why it can be hard to change. It is not that you are lazy, necessarily, it is that your brain has changed and needs to be rewired. However, each time you engage in a behaviour or thought you want to avoid, you are offered the opportunity to make a different choice and strengthen different connections. That kind of change takes effort, so pick your spots. You can change almost anything you want about your mind, but not all things will be worth changing. You have limited time and resources just like everyone else.

Understanding that, when it comes to your own thoughts and habits, change is possible but difficult is exactly why I have divided this book into (mostly) independent sections. There are many possible things you could decide to improve about your life, but some will be more worthwhile pursuits than others. Prioritize, and do not feel guilty. Be realistic about what you want to attempt, and commit to seeing it through.

Sources

Hanson, R. (2014). 'How to grow the good in your brain'. *Greater Good: The Science of a Meaningful Life.* http://greatergood.berkeley.edu/article/item/how_to_grow_the_good_in_your_brain

Bethune, B. (2015). 'How you brain can heal itself'. *Macleans Magazine.* www.macleans.ca/society/health/how-your-brain-heals-itself/

Dubuc, B. (2006). 'Plasticity in neural networks'. *The Brain From Top to Bottom.* www.thebrain.mcgill.ca/flash/i/i_07/i_07_m/i_07_m_tra/i_07_m_tra.html

BUSY AND BARRIERS

THE QUESTION OF PRIVILEGE

Some of you may be reading this and wondering, "What planet is she from? How could she assume that I would have enough time/money/support to do any of this? I have to work part-time, I have to commute for hours, I have to take care of my siblings. I don't have the energy or mental space to find my niche. All of the things she is talking about are nice things for privileged kids to do so that their already-successful trajectories can be made a little more shiny."

You might be correct, but that is only part of the truth. I hope that students of all kinds can benefit from this book. I have tried to bake in an understanding of the challenges that many of you might be facing.

I want to be honest; I come from a place of privilege. I was born into a developed country with a peaceful political situation. I was lovingly raised by a supportive and stable family. We weren't stinking rich, but we never worried about money. I have never held a retail job, or had to focus on anything besides my schooling. I have had a lot of time to think, a lot of energy with which to experiment, and a lot of opportunities to learn. I know that many of the defining factors of my life were out of my control. The lottery of birth afforded me a winning ticket. I recognize that most people on this planet, and even maybe most of you who are reading this may not have gotten as good of a ticket. It is not fair, and I have committed myself to trying to make my lucky life useful. I feel responsible to share the result of my past decade of experimenting. What I have tried to do is to provide shortcuts to patterns of thought and action that have served me well in a variety of contexts (school, work, and my personal life).

I understand as well that my techniques and tactics focus mostly on changing the individual rather than the system. I tend to advise you to find ways you can align yourselves with the broader forces in your life. But what if these broader forces are directing you towards poverty, or a constricting kind of life? What if your parents have clear desires for your future? What if your entire family expects a certain destiny from you? What if women in your neighbourhood or culture are expected to fulfil traditional roles? In short, what if the forces of life are stacked against your goals?

Let it be clear that I do not recommend submitting. What I do recommend is a strategic approach to your life, regardless of your obstacles and goals. The finite nature of willpower is especially relevant for readers in challenging situations. If you try to fight every battle, you will be exhausted and crushed. What I recommend is radical patience, a term I first encountered when reading about bicycle activists in the San Francisco. Bicyclists and car drivers are notoriously antagonistic towards each other, each believing that the other group is misguided and inconsiderate. Activist Chris Carlsson realized that each side's anger was destructive. Barring a catastrophic event that killed all car-drivers, the greener, better world that cyclists envisioned would have to involve everyone. In the interests of progress, it was better to seek to bridge the two sides rather than continue to divide them. Cyclists would be more successful if they showcased the benefits of cycling without threatening car-drivers; for example, by organizing peaceful rides that did not result in confrontations between the two groups.

What does this have to do with you? Even if you do not agree with a system or a group of people, if they are powerful or numerous, you cannot ignore them, or turn them into your enemies. You need to find a way to be disruptive without being threatening, or find a way to use their size and momentum against them. It is a delicate art.

Still, the most important battle you will fight lies within yourself. Your environment has a way of soaking into your head. You may have invisible assumptions that subtly shape your behaviour. Exposing yourself to different people and perspectives is one way to turn the invisible visible. Films and novels are easy ways to do this. Try to see the world from the eyes of others to understand what makes you different. Then, decide whether these beliefs are helpful or harmful.

Removing or replacing them is a topic we covered in our section on Identifying and Challenging Your Assumptions.

Sources

Carlsson, C. (1993). 'Radical patience.' *San Francisco Critical Mass.* www.scorcher.org/cmhistory/patience.html

Conversations with Azimi, F. (2015, June).

BARRIERS

For some people, high school is the best of times, for more, it is the worst of times, and for most people, it is both at the same time. As one of my friends said to me, "It's this strange time in your life where you are expected to be independent and mature enough to make choices about your future, and at the same time, you have to ask permission to use the bathroom when you're in class." We need to talk about this. You need to know that I understand the mixture of freedom and structure in your life.

As a student, so much of your day is structured. You have a set start, end and lunch time, you have to attend classes, and you probably have other responsibilities once the school day is done. This is a book about optimizing different aspects of your life, and you might feel that you don't have the time or mental space to even begin to think about changing anything. You're probably right.

One of the most memorable lessons I learned in my first few weeks of university is that time is static. When I was being welcomed into my university program, the program administrator had us write down the number '168' on a piece of paper. You might recognize this number as the product of seven and 24. It's the number of hours in a week. All of us students estimated how many hours we wanted to spend studying, exercising, volunteering, and working. Once we subtracted these from 168, she reminded us that we need eight hours of sleep a day, and probably three for meals. Most of us were now in negative time. Our schedules were impossible. I have a feeling that many of you reading this book have schedules that skirt the edge of impossible. Challenging yourself in this way can help you build time management skills, but it often does not allow you to make bigger changes to your life (such as improving the way you study) that could result in enormous benefits down the line.

I am not telling you to immediately stop everything you are doing

BARRIERS

(though if you still feel this way at the end of this section, read our series on Quitting!), but I do think it is important to take stock of your constraints. Where does your time and energy go to right now? Why are you involved in each pursuit? What skills are you learning? Are you required to continue all of them? Which would be easiest to get out of? Which would you miss the most? A perfect format to begin to tease out your involvements is a table with seven columns. Label them with the days of the week, and draw out blocks to show where you are spending your time. Ask yourself the series of questions I threw at you, and if any red flags come up (*ie* "I don't know why I am doing this," "I feel like I should do this, but I am not learning much from it," "I could easily leave this but just haven't"), colour the block red, and decide what you will do about it. With a yellow highlighter, colour activities that are currently not giving you much of a return on your effort, but that you think could be vastly improved with a little effort. Maybe your math and biology classes seem like a waste of time now, but you know that if you were able to better link them with your goal of becoming a psychologist, you would have a more rewarding experience in both of them. Save the green marker for activities you are proud that you engage in, activities that give you so much energy, learning and fuel for life that you feel you would be lost without them. Congratulate yourself for treating yourself well. In a world where people tend to judge your worth based on how much you have produced and achieved, taking care of yourself is an act of defiance that needs celebrating.

Now, look at your week. What colour dominates? Whichever one does, that is okay. We're not done. Our next task is to figure out why that colour is dominating. Let's say most of your blocks are coloured red. It's time to look at the other barriers and constraints in your life. Perhaps some of the necessities for empowered living are missing. Think about your environment at home and at school. Do you feel supported? Do you feel neglected? Do you feel victimized? Sometimes, the most effective thing you can do in response to a harmful environment is to remove yourself. A close friend of mine moved to his grandmother's house for the last few years of high school because his family situation was unhealthy. If you feel like the problems in your environment are beyond what you can handle, there is no shame in choosing to protect and nourish yourself. I cannot promise you that there will always be an easy way out, but I encourage you to at least look for one. You deserve to be helped and supported. Ask for both.

Perhaps things are not so bad as to require you to leave, but you still feel a lack of support from the people who are closest to you. Maybe your parents have very strict ideas about what it means to be successful in high school. Or, maybe they have to work so much that you don't have a chance to spend very much good quality time with them. Be honest with yourself about the unique set of challenges you have to face. Try to think about how you might offset or overcome them.

Once you have thought about the influence that others and the environment have on you, and you have tried to diminish these to the best of your ability, the main limiting factor on your own success is you. Your beliefs, habits and mindset can hurt you, but they can also help you, and they are in your control. The rest of this book is about how you can better understand and develop yourself. To avoid blaming or congratulating yourself for the consequences of factors outside of your control, it is important to begin by understanding your context.

[REJECT]
THE CULT OF
BUSY

CULT OF BUSY

Reader, you were born into a difficult world. There are more people on this planet than there have ever been before. Economies are global, not local, and you've been put in the position of competing for what seems like a shrinking pot of opportunities. You might think that the only way to ensure you are successful is to simply do more of the things that have made other people successful: work harder, study harder, and become more and more involved in your community. Where I went to high school and university, some of my classmates would pride themselves on their busyness. Being overinvolved was a badge they could use to show how well they were living. Until recently, I also fell into this crowd. I thought that the quantity of activities and their diversity was a better metric for success than what actually happened during my days. It took me until my third year of university to realize that if I aligned more of my activities, I could achieve more in the end and have a better experience in the process.

Piling on extracurriculars can teach you time-management skills, but being involved in too many activities can pull you in so many directions that the vector sum is zero. You may build some skills in a variety of areas, but you will get nowhere near as far as you can if you choose to focus on a few domains. There is a balance to strike between challenging your organizational skills and getting meaningful results from these activities, but what's most important is rejecting the narrative that says that the quantity of work you do is what will make you successful. As I learned the hard way, this plan is a recipe for exhaustion rather than success. It is a recipe for never thinking critically about your habits or the world you live in. Being overinvolved and over-achieving is inefficient, uninspired and unhealthy. With a little more strategic thinking, you can find your niche and excel authentically.

You will also start to influence others to think and live as you do. Perhaps that is one solution to the problem of global competition.

Instead of directly competing with so many other people, by refusing to stray from the traditional narrative of what makes a successful person, you decide to differentiate yourself. You refuse to believe that there are not enough niches for all of us, and you refuse to compromise the quality of your life to get to wherever you need to go.

How does this perspective apply to academics? Wouldn't it make sense to coast in most courses, and only make a real effort in the few in which you can see direct links to your future aspirations? Unfortunately, it is not that simple. Your aspirations will direct your behaviour on this front. If you want to attend a highly selective university program, even if you are planning to specialize in physics, all of your marks probably matter. If you are planning to go to culinary school, skills you probably will not be able to learn in the classroom might matter a lot more.

Rejecting the cult of busy means questioning whether there is only one way to succeed, and using your critical and creative thinking skills to find a personalized path. Doing so allows you to avoid redundant or irrelevant components of the traditional path, freeing up time and mental energy. It also means that you can much more easily draw from intrinsic motivation.

Challenging the narrative of busy will only get harder as you get older. The more that people come to associate you with a particular pattern of thinking and acting, the harder it will be to change their perceptions of you. Also, the longer you think and act a certain way, the harder it is to change. If you are choosing an alternative route, the sooner you can show results, the more easily people will start to support you. I am lucky enough to be part of a family that trusts my judgment, but I know that other people's parents and supports have very clear and traditional ideas of what it means to be successful. Even if it is not possible to change your path immediately, at least think about it. Devote some mental space to imagining how things will be different. Then, when an opportunity arises (one activity comes to a natural close, or you are faced with a choice that will define your future years), you will be prepared to act. Don't dream of having it all. Dream of doing fewer things, but doing them better than anyone you know.

WRONG CHOICE?

WASTING MORE $/ / WON'T MAKE IT RIGHT!

QUITTING, SUNK COSTS, AND OPPORTUNITY COSTS

"We fail when we are distracted by the tasks we don't have the guts to quit." - Seth Godin

"If at first you don't succeed, try, try again. Then quit. There's no point in being a damn fool about it." - W. C. Fields

If you are a middle class kid, life can seem pretty sweet. You have support (financial and hopefully otherwise) from your parents, your material comforts are taken care of, and it can seem like your dreams are in reach. With hard work, and few barriers, so long as you don't give up, you are bound to reach them. This idea is repeated so much that it has become conventional wisdom. However, at least for a certain group of dreamers, the research of Sudhir Venkatesh, a sociologist at Columbia University, challenges this conventional wisdom. He found that when you compare the lives of upper middle class males who were selected in the Major League Baseball draft to upper middle class kids in general, you see a striking difference a decade later. Very few of the players who were drafted are in the major league and successful. Most of them are making only about $25,000 a year, piecing together part-time jobs in the off-season, and playing baseball with a lower-rung team for the rest of the time. In contrast, their upper middle class peers were definitely doing much better one decade later. They had above average incomes, good careers, and lived in safe neighbourhoods. Perhaps some were following their dreams, and perhaps still more had quit ones that they realized would take more to achieve than they were willing to pay. Perseverance might be the key to success in a domain, but that perseverance comes at a cost. In many scenarios, the cost of persevering is not worth the payoff. There is nothing wrong with quitting, so long as you do it for the right reasons, and at the right time.

If you could see different possible futures with perfect clarity, you would never have to quit. Before you decided whether to lace up your running shoes on your first training session, you would be able to look with your magic periscope one year later to the finish line of the marathon and see whether you would complete it. After your first date with a new paramour, you could use that little periscope to jump to your relationship's break-up, and judge whether the experience was worth it. Luckily and unluckily for us, this is not the case. Our lives are full of uncertainty. The future is murky, which makes living exciting, but also can drum up anxiety. We can never quite be sure what is around the corner, and we live in fear of making a decision that we might regret.

This uncertain future is what makes quitting so hard sometimes. With the road ahead so misty, we tend to look back to the past. We obsess over how hard we have already worked in pursuit of this goal, skill, job, or relationship. We fear that walking away now is a surefire way to waste our resources. And yet, each time we convince ourselves to stick it out a little bit longer, the more time and effort we spend, and the more compelled we feel to continue a bad course of action. The thing is, if we are not going to win a war, sending more troops to die in honour of those who have already lost their lives is a foolish thing to do. Yet, it seems emotionally right. Backing out of a conflict when so much has already been lost amounts to admitting that we were wrong, and that all the death and carnage that has already occurred has happened for no good reason. Of course, it is a terrible situation, but how will continuing to fight a losing war make anything better? It is only a short-term balm for our raw emotions. This trap doesn't just happen in wartime. It can happen when you are trying to figure out whether to dump your long-term boyfriend (two years of your life!), or if you are considering whether to stop playing competitive chess (eight years of practice!). When it does, psychologists call it the sunk cost fallacy, because, the reality is, these costs are 'sunk'. No matter what you do, they will never come back.

How do you avoid being swayed by the sunk cost fallacy? You can start to look for it in others. Whenever someone offers sunk time or effort as a reason for continuing a course of action, a little red flag should start waving in your head. Ask the person (or yourself, if the person making the sunk cost reference is you) whether he would make a different choice if he had just begun whatever activity to which he is referring. If the answer is different, your intuition was correct.

Battling the sunk cost fallacy requires familiarizing yourself with another kind of cost. Economists love this one. It's called the opportunity cost, and it pushes you to ask the question "What else could I be doing?". Of course, there are many other things you could be doing, but when determining the opportunity cost, you limit yourself to the next best option. If you are thinking of ending a relationship, the opportunity cost of staying in your current relationship is the fun and enjoyment you could have being single, or the intimacy, excitement and love you could enjoy in a new relationship (whatever one you value more). When you compare your opportunity cost to your current returns, whichever one is higher is the one you should probably stick with. Note that the opportunity cost is a measurement that looks at the present and towards the future. It is a useful balance for the backward-looking sunk cost fallacy. After all, the past has passed. There is no need to let it control our future any more than we would like it to.

Sources

Hard, B. (2013). 'Seth Godin's 'The dip'. *Constantly Learning.* www.bretthard.in/2013/01/the-dip-book-review-seth-godin/

Dubner, S. (2011). 'The upside of quitting'. *Freakonomics Radio.* www.freakonomics.com/2011/09/30/the-upside-of-quitting-full-transcript/

Moffat, M. (2015). 'What are opportunity costs'. *About Economics.* www.economics.about.com/od/opportunitycosts/f/opportunitycost.htm

Davis, Z. (2009). 'Sunk cost fallacy'. *Less Wrong.* www.lesswrong.com/lw/at/sunk_cost_fallacy/

THE DARK SIDE OF QUITTING

THE DARK SIDE OF QUITTING, AND WHAT TO DO ABOUT IT

Our previous section on quitting may have left you with the impression that quitting is sometimes a necessary step that frees you to pursue a better goal. What we neglected to cover was that often, quitting is not clean or simple. There may be people relying on you. Simply disappearing from view one day is not going to bode well for your relationships, whether they are working or personal ones. Knowing when to quit, and knowing how to quit are two different things.

Knowing how to quit properly is a weakness of mine. I have been working on it lately, and here is what I wish I could tell myself when I was in high school. The first thing is to be careful what you promise to people. It is easy to let optimism and a desire to please others lead you to tell them you are committed to an activity for the long haul, but if even a part of you is doubtful, give yourself an out. Commit to a short-term 'testing out' period, after which you can reassess whether you have made the right choice. The easiest time to quit is before you have gotten invested in something. Always ask for time to think when someone asks you to commit to something or join an organization. This buffer of time will allow your more analytical System 2 to determine whether you can really take up more responsibilities, and it will prevent System 1 from trying to please the person in the moment.

The second thing is to understand how quitting will affect others, and take steps to minimize the fallout. If you are volunteering on a charity committee, that means finding a replacement for your role. It also means communicating clearly about your intentions. Quite a few times, I have tried to 'sneak out' of roles by withdrawing slowly, rather than telling people my honest intentions. I know that these choices damaged some of my working relationships, and if I could go back, I would be much more transparent.

The third thing is to know how to be honest with yourself about whether you are going to finish something. The danger with becoming someone who quits things is that you might start to quit things you really should have stayed with. Quitting, if not properly managed, can erode your ability to finish anything, even things you really care about. How can you be a quitter and a finisher at the same time? Scott Young, a blogger who became famous for finishing MIT's four-year online computer science curriculum in one year, has written about a strategy for dealing with this dilemma. He recommends mentally classifying your undertakings as either commitments or experiments. Commitments are things that you are definitely going to finish, no matter what happens. Experiments are things that you are trying, but that you give yourself permission to quit after a certain point if they are not working out the way you wanted them to. That last part is important. Experiments are short-term, and have built-in decision points where you are allowed to end them. Having this mental distinction will probably make you more careful about what tasks you take on as commitments, and it might free you to try some things you would not have tried otherwise, now that you can mentally frame them as experiments.

Quit carefully, quit gracefully, and finish what you care about.

Sources

Young, S. (2015). 'How to build the habit of finishing what you start'. *Scott H Young's Blog.* www.scotthyoung.com/blog/2015/04/01/finish-what-you-start/

FIRST DRAFTS RULE!

FIRST DRAFTS

RULE!

DOING HARD THINGS

When it comes to creative activities like writing and problem solving, I find that greatness comes from iteration. A craggy mess of rock can become a beautiful sculpture after rounds of careful chipping, so long as its internal structure is good. I used to be embarrassed of what I would produce as a first draft, whether it was an essay, or my first crack at organizing my day. I finally saw the beauty in these ugly masses of rock after I tried to create my first comic book. I had never done anything like it before, so I was faced with countless decisions. What images should I use to convey this idea? In what order? How should I arrange the panels on each page? What colours should I use?

When you are faced with a complex task, it is usually impossible to conceptualize how all of your choices will function together. Trying to do so can result in what is called 'paralysis by analysis.' When this tendency combines with perfectionism, you become your own worst enemy. If you are writing an essay, you might have a terribly difficult time deciding how to start the essay. For each word you write, you might erase two more. Now, this strategy might succeed eventually, but I do not think that it is the most efficient approach. It was not the one I chose to use for my comic book. I knew that I did not have enough time to agonize over the details from the very start of the project.

So, what *did* I do with my comic book? I built a schedule for myself that included deadlines for three drafts, and adjusted my expectations for their quality accordingly. The first draft was full of rough sketches, and had the words totally separate from the images. Everything was in pencil. Keeping the components of this draft as minimal as possible allowed me to focus on the overall flow of the story. Did the different chapters work together? Were some of my motifs too repetitive? I gave myself permission to draw messily, and write in short forms. Once I completed the draft, I set it aside for a weekend, and then I tore into it with all the critical force I could muster. I cut out and repasted different panels, I eliminated entire chapters, and I reworded huge sections. Editing was exhilarating, both because I knew how much I was improving my comic, but also because I was glad I had not put more effort into the panels that had to be eliminated.

I probably engaged in just as much critical thinking as I would have if I had taken the first approach, but by separating criticizing from creating, I enhanced my experience. I found that waiting until I had finished the first version of my task, and allowing myself to take a break before reviewing, I felt better throughout the whole process, and I didn't have to sacrifice the quality of my work.

Since this project, I have adapted this approach more broadly. While I am writing any kind of draft, I give myself permission to make mistakes. So long as I understand the kernel of the idea that lies behind a vague phrase or cliché sentence, I can make peace with that section and move on. This self-permission lets me enjoy the first stage of the writing, and it also gives me some low-hanging fruit to correct when I start editing. Interestingly, knowing that I have some incentive to make small mistakes encourages me to write more freely. As soon as I stop expecting what I am writing to be perfect, I free myself to write more naturally and with a calmer internal state. I find that this state can produce better ideas and turns of phrase than my overly analytical state of mind.

Moreover, when I get to the editing stage, I find that it is easier to make huge changes to a piece of work because I do not feel as though I have already invested all of the time I wanted to spend on the project. I am more bold with my red pen, and the project is better for it.

The reason I think that separating the creating from the criticizing works so well is that it is a way to deal with the complexity of the task. Much like we will discuss in our section about Turning the Internal External, creating an entire first draft allows you to see how different components are interacting with each other. You do not have to hold anything in your memory; you can merely observe the real specimen and let the higher level functions of your brain take centre stage.

SATISFICING

OR

?

?

MAXIMIZING?

!

?

MAXIMIZING?

Who do you think are happier: the people who try to make the best possible decisions, or the people who look for things that are simply 'good-enough'? Psychologist Barry Schwartz has found that it's the 'good-enough' seekers. He calls them 'satisficers', partly because they tend to be more satisfied with their choices. They have a set of criteria that need to be met, and they stop looking as soon as they find something that meets all of them. The other group, called maximizers, go through option after option and gorge on information until they make themselves sick. Even after they make a decision, they are often agonized by the thought that a better option might be out there.

Satisficers have made peace with the fact that to win whatever war they are fighting, they may need to lose a few smaller battles. They have stopped chasing perfection because they know it is a distraction, something that requires more energy than it returns. I bring up this distinction because I am wagering that many of the people reading this book lie closer to the side of maximizing than satisficing. I know that I definitely did when I was in high school.

Some of you may be arguing, quite rightly, that the happiness that satisficers feel does not necessarily mean that they have made better decisions. Someone who maximizes will tend to find better deals than someone who satisfices. Yet, the important fact about satisficers is that they have a list of criteria that must be met before they make a decision. The difference between satisficers and maximizers is how far above "good enough" the maximizers will venture. Whether that difference is worth the additional effort and negative emotions is something you will have to decide for yourself. As a recent convert from maximizing all the time to satisficing most of the time, I can tell you that the marginally better outcomes I experienced when maximizing didn't outweigh the anxiety it caused me.

Maximizers also tend to take longer to make decisions. Satisficing is much faster, and usually protects you from languishing in the planning stages of any action, whether it is buying ingredients for a cake, or deciding how to spend your winter break.

You might find it strange that I am telling you to go for what is 'good enough' in a book that is supposed to be about realizing your full potential. To me, it's not so strange. You are a person with limited time and energy. If you want to 'maximize' in the areas where the extra benefits will really matter, you will have to streamline the rest of your life.

This book is an inventory of advice, practices and suggestions, but I do not intend them to be fuel for a perfectionist fire. The last thing I would want to happen is for you to be so busy thinking about how you can use a school project to your best advantage that you end up wasting most of your time in hypotheticals. One way to balance the value-adding possibilities of the tips in this book is to 'book off' only a little bit of time at the beginning of the project to consider what one tactic you will use. Once you find one that you would like to try, choose it. Tell yourself that a completed experiment is better than a thousand hypotheses. Commit to using this tactic in the project. If you cannot find an appropriate hack to try, make peace with the result and move on. There is no shame in 'good enough,' because an opportunity to be 'excellent' may lie around the corner, waiting for you to have the time and energy to seize it.

Sources

Bernstein, E. (2014). 'How you make decisions says a lot about how happy you are'. *Wall Street Journal*. www.wsj.com/articles/how-you-make-decisions-says-a-lot-about-how-happy-you-are-1412614997

HOW TO EAT A PLANE

How do you write a book? When I started this project, I had no idea. All that I knew was that I needed to write about 40,000 words. Without a plan, this large project was looming over me like one of those little stormclouds that follows cartoon characters. Then, I remembered Michel Lotito. This Frenchman ate 18 bicycles, an airplane, 15 shopping carts, and even six chandeliers. It did not so much matter *why* he ate any of these things (apparently he had a condition that caused him to crave eating metal), but *how*. He ate them one bite and swallow at a time. "One bite at a time," is a humourous answer for the relatively obscure question "How do you eat an airplane?", but it is also accurate advice.

Taking a page from Lotito's book, I calculated how many full days I would have at my disposal to write the first draft, and divided the total words I needed by these available dates. After adding in some contingency time at the end, I realized that I could write about 1500 words a day and reach my total comfortably. To make these bites even smaller, I divided them into two 750-word pieces. Suddenly, 40,000 words did not seem so intimidating. All I needed to think about on a daily basis was hitting my quota. I built in time for review once I had completed a significant chunk of the writing, but otherwise, my solution was very similar to Loito. He used to break up his metal meals into pieces small enough to swallow, and then take a large glass of water and gulp them down until he had eaten one kilogram.

Why am I telling you this? My experience with writing this book emphasizes how impossible things can become possible if we package them artfully. One of the few maxims I repeat to myself is that "You can do a lot when you work little by little." If I tried to book five days and write this book, I could not do it, or at least could not do it well.

It is easier to maintain focus for shorter periods of time than it is for longer ones. We work far more efficiently when we parcel out tasks.

ONE bite
AT A time

Breaking things into bite-sized chunks that are almost too easy *not* to do can also help us overcome the intimidation we feel when faced with monumental tasks. Human beings are suckers for rewards, and the satisfaction we feel when we have completed a task that we set for ourselves (even if the task itself is small) can provide motivation to keep going. After a while, realizing how far you have come is sure to provide even more motivation to finish the next bit. Even if you fall off the wagon, or miss some of your targets, focusing on that next small task provides a friendly way to get back on track.

This same approach can be applied to studying for exams. Notes are much easier to make one week at a time, rather than trying to review every section a few days before the examination. Periodically testing yourself puts you in much better shape than pushing all the reviewing to the end. I find that adopting this technique improves your own experience of whatever work you are doing. With clear boundaries in place about the scope and effort required for each step, you have almost nothing to worry about except the work itself. You are more likely to be able to focus on the small task itself, and more likely to enjoy it.

The next time you have a dream and then immediately dismiss it because it seems too impractical, I would encourage you to think about whether you can approach it like you would if you wanted to swallow an airplane. Can you turn a mountain into a series of steps? If you can, start climbing. Good luck!

Sources

Ciotti, G. '5 scientific ways to build habits that stick.' *99u.* www.99u.com/articles/17123/5-scientific-ways-to-build-habits-that-stick

Lorenzo, T. (2012, October 1). 'Michel loito: the man who ate an airplane and everything else'. *Tailgate Fan.* http://tailgatefan.cbslocal.com/2012/10/01/michel-lotito-the-man-who-ate-an-airplane-and-everything-else/

PARKINSON'S LAW

"Work expands to fill the time allotted for its completion." – Cyril Northcote Parkinson.

Boy, is he right! If you give yourself six hours to study for a test, you'll take the full six (probably including some internet breaks!). And yet, if you give yourself four hours, it will take four. Will the quality be exactly the same? In my experience, your performance will be hard to distinguish. Of course, if you give yourself three minutes to write a research essay, this law will fail. It's less of a law than it is an observation. We tend to pad our working time with distracted time, and sometimes overestimate the amount of effort that will be required to complete our tasks because we take into account this padding.

I've heard new mothers refer to this law when they say they can't believe that they used to think ten minutes was not enough time to do anything. I won't be a parent for a long time, but I have had a parallel experience. When I started my first serious relationship, I was surprised to see that although I was spending a significant chunk of my weekend on hikes or cooking or at galleries, I was still able to complete all of my school and extracurricular work. I didn't even feel substantially more stressed. I had a good reason for focusing, and so I could focus. Time was elastic, or so it seemed.

All that you need to follow my lead is a very good reason to work smarter. Maybe it is so that you can play in a band, or excel at a sports team. Maybe you want to volunteer in a science museum, or you need to work a part-time job. Maybe you want to spend more time with your boyfriend or girlfriend. The point is, these extracurricular involvements can actually help, rather than hinder, your school work. They push you into a higher gear. When there are others to whom you are accountable, suddenly deadlines can't just be pushed back

SO FILL YOUR LIFE

WITH JUST ENOUGH
TO MAKE YOU
HAPPY & EFFICIENT

because you made bad choices. It's a great incentive to build good habits.

I am not advocating for stuffing your life with everything you can think of. With too many tasks to keep track of, you start to lose all of the benefits of Parkinson's law. I would recommend doing a few things that you really care about, and doing them well.

Sources

N.a. (1955). 'Parkinson's Law'. *The Economist.* www.economist.com/node/14116121

PLANNING FALLACY AND ILLUSORY SUPERIORITY

Our minds are fantastic pieces of equipment. There's a reason that the task of constructing genuine artificial intelligence is one of herculean difficulty. Some things are effortless for us, like distinguishing an apple from a baseball, but are very difficult to program. And yet, despite the awesomeness of our minds, we have cognitive biases. Think of them as purposeful little bugs in our mental software. Some of these heuristics are useful in our modern lives, but the planning fallacy is not. It's just plain unhelpful. The planning fallacy is one of the reasons why you find yourself running to get the bus, or typing feverishly late into the evening on the night before your paper is due. The planning fallacy is a mental bug that causes people to chronically underestimate the amount of time tasks will take. Why do we do this?

One reason is that we tend to view tasks holistically rather than in detail. We try to estimate how long it will take us to finish our essays, we are not likely to separate carrying out research, keeping records of sources, brainstorming a thesis, creating an outline, writing the first draft, editing, and creating the final version. We are more likely to think of one giant activity of 'paper writing.' Julia Galef of the Center for Applied Rationality argues that because we only perceive of one large task rather than several smaller ones, we are likely to underestimate the probability of something going wrong. When you are presented with seven different stages, it seems more probable that a delay could occur for at least one of the steps. Yet, when you are faced with one 'mega-stage', it seems less likely that there could be any deviation from the 'normal time taken.' A research study showed that when people were prompted to break a task down into detailed steps, they estimated the duration of the task more accurately than people who were allowed to come to their estimations intuitively.

Another reason is that human beings are a curious mixture of optimistic and forgetful. Even if we have done a task before, and remember how long it took, we tend to assume that things will move faster this time around. We tend to assume that nothing will go wrong, and that the power to succeed lies squarely in our capable hands. It's not necessarily surprising that people tend to be overconfident about their own effectiveness. It's actually the result of another of those pesky mental software bugs called illusory superiority, or the 'above average' fallacy. We tend to assume that we are 'above average' in many domains (looks, intelligence, skill, and even fitness), despite the fact that if everyone is above 'average,' that average cannot be correct!

Yet, there is a way to get around this overconfidence. A 2012 study done by Dr. Buehler at Wilfrid Laurier University showed that when people were told to mentally picture the task like an 'outsider' would do, they tended to come up with more reasonable estimates than people who maintained their 'insider' perspectives. The 'above average' effect vanishes when we start to consider other people. We are much more accurate at judging their performance than we are with our own, because we are more likely to assume that others will be derailed by delays or other random occurrences.

Even if you have fallen victim to the planning fallacy before, you now have the knowledge to avoid it in the future. Breaking down large tasks into smaller pieces before you estimate the total time you will require, consulting past experiences with similar tasks, and taking an 'outsider' perspective (or, better yet, talking to a real outsider with relevant past experience) can all help you avoid last-minute panic. Follow these steps and you will truly be 'above average' when it comes to your planning skills – I promise!

Sources

Ghose, T. (2013). 'Why we're all above average'. *LiveScience*. www.livescience.com/26914-why-we-are-all-above-average.html

Reddy, S. (2015). 'We know why you are always late.' *The Wall Street Journal*. www.wsj.com/articles/we-know-why-youre-always-late-1422900180

Galef, J. 'A day late and a dollar short: the planning fallacy explained.' www.bigthink.com/in-their-own-words/why-you-cant-plan

TURN THE
internal
EXTERNAL
376
×14

TURNING THE INTERNAL EXTERNAL

A few years ago, I was in Pondicherry, India, learning from a woman who had spent eight years of her life living on the streets to work with children who had experienced trauma. I sat quietly as she placed smooth stones in my hands. I turned them over and read what had been painted on them: 'anger', 'happiness', and 'sadness'.

"We tell the children to use these stones to represent what is going on in their minds and hearts. Then, we tell them to move the stones like they want to move their feelings. We help them gain control." These stones connected the physical world with intangible parts of the human experience. I was in awe of the simplicity and ingenuity of this idea.

You and I are much more fortunate than traumatized street children in India, but we still carry a jumble of thoughts and emotions in our heads. Our minds are dynamic and organic. Trying to understand what is really going on inside them in real time is almost impossible. It would be like trying to understand how a dog runs by having it sprint by you repeatedly. Memory is also notoriously fallible. You will probably learn about this neat bit of cognitive psychology at some point in your life, but when we remember something, we are actually re-creating the memory, which means re-firing all the neurons. It is relatively easy for a mistake to occur and for us to save over the original memory with a changed one.

Where am I going with this line of thought? We need static representations to accurately understand the mechanics of our dynamic minds. Whether it is through painted stones, journal pages, or a document on a computer screen, you need a canvas to represent your mind. Why? Understanding and mapping your thoughts and emotions is the first step to learning from them and shaping them. These external representations of internal processes are vital parts of understanding and living well with yourself. Keeping a journal, having a whiteboard you write on, or even using sticky notes to represent different ideas can all be wonderful ways to take control of the slippery goings-on inside your head. They can be especially helpful when you are confused and emotional.

Developing a habit of reflecting can go a long way. To take control of what's inside, bring it outside, and engage with it constructively. It is probably the single most important thing you can do as a young person. Understanding your dreams, weaknesses, secret powers, and fears will help you make better choices.

External representations come in many forms. I am drawn to visual forms (give me a blank page, and large markers and I am quite happy), but for you it might help to walk as you think. You might need to write, or you might need to talk to someone else. What is more important is that you find a way to transpose your thoughts into a different medium so that you can create objective distance between your thoughts and yourself. (It might sound counter-intuitive that you can be something apart from your thoughts, but our section on System 1 and System 2 should be of some help there!)

A crucial element of a successful reflection session is focus. You should try to find a place that will not distract you. Libraries are great options, and depending on the weather, a park could be very calming. Even your bedroom could work in a pinch. Our brains tend to associate the context in which we learn something (be it a concept or a habit), so try to pick a location that will be easy for you to visit regularly. I would encourage you to reflect at the end of large chunks of your experience (the end of a school term, the end of a month, for example), and also on an as-needed basis. Regular reflection will help you build the skills you need to deal with problems as they arise. From personal experience, if you keep a record of what you learned from these sessions, they are such a valuable resource for you to look back on. When I read some of my reflections from years ago, I am struck by such love and self-compassion. I am reminded of how much I have grown and how many challenges I have overcome. I am re-inspired to grapple with the problems that haven't gone away.

Externalizing your internal world is also a way to keep an accurate history of your life. This record is one of the most precious things you will ever create. Only you can create it. This record is something no one else can ever hope to imitate. It can help remind you that your life is rich, full, and deep, even if the external world seems boring. Always remember that inside, you are a being of staggering complexity and beauty.

ORGANIZE

ORGANIZING YOUR MIND

I was going to start this section with a glib reference to the notoriously short memory span of a goldfish (three seconds), but, being the diligent writer I am, I first thought I would find a reputable source for this information. It turns out that goldfish have a memory of up to three months, and they can even be trained to navigate through mazes! While goldfish everywhere deserve a sincere apology for being the butt of so many memory jokes, the fact remains that memory is fallible. Whether you are a goldfish or a person, your memory has a (relatively) fixed capacity. Most people can hold between four and seven 'chunks' in their working (short term) memory. These chunks could be simple, like a number, or they could be more complicated, like the items on a grocery list. These chunks could even contain chunks, which is exactly what we do when we try to remember longer phone numbers. The number 416439000 becomes 416 439 0000 (call it if you want to order pizza in Canada!). It's unlikely that you would be able to fit your entire schedule of tasks, even for the day, in your short term memory. Even if you could learn from the elaborate visualizing techniques of World Memory Championship winners (a topic we cover in our section on Mental Imagery and Spatial Memory), I doubt that it would be very practical.

Maintaining control over your life demands organization. Proper planning can allow you to take advantage of emerging opportunities (because you won't be running behind on your 'normal' tasks), track and reward your progress, and make time for healthy and nourishing activities. You might think that planning is only for secretaries, but there is a reason secretaries are paid money to plan for other people. Having a well-managed schedule frees your mind for more important things. You might be able to be more mindful throughout the day, engage more fully with friends, or think about your path in life if you spent less time stumbling from activity to activity, or freaking out about the assignment you forgot was due tomorrow.

All that I think you need is a calendar and a priority list. Note that I say priority rather than 'to-do'. Many lists of the 'to-do' sort become unmanageable and overwhelming. A few years ago, I read about an alternative process to the to-do list on Cal Newport's (productivity and quality of life-obsessed university student turned professor) blog Study Hacks, and I have used it with great results. Cal advises people to create a list of tasks, but then to create a mini-timeline of their day, and slot in the tasks with a time estimate into the open areas. Very quickly, this process provides you with an idea of how much you can probably accomplish, and, just as importantly, it gives you a structure to your work. There will be fewer decisions to make during your day, so you will be able to focus more on finishing the tasks and moving towards your goals.

I find that having a calendar over my desk with important deadlines (for assignments, exams, or projects) listed helps remind me of the longer-term tasks that can sometimes slip under the radar. Splitting larger long-term tasks into smaller chunks (as you can read about in our One Bite at a Time section) and putting these mini-deadlines on the calendar is a great way to avoid procrastination, and the dreaded all-nighter the day before the deadline.

Getting organized might not be sexy, but it will free you up to be more adventurous, more in control, more at peace, and more empowered. What's the downside to that?

Sources

N.a. (2009). 'Three second memory myth: fish show they can remember things for five months'. *The Daily Mail.* www.dailymail.co.uk/sciencetech/article-1106884/Three-second-memory-myth-Fish-remember-months.html

Newport, C. (2007). 'Don't use a daily to-do list'. *Study Hacks Blog: Decoding Patterns of Success.* www.calnewport.com/blog/2007/12/03/monday-master-class-dont-plan-your-day-with-a-to-do-list/

THRIVING IN COMPLEXITY

INTERNAL LOCUS OF control

INTERNAL LOCUS OF CONTROL

You may have thought that Fate versus Free Will was a duel that would never leave your English literature classroom, but it turns out that your opinion on this matter might determine your happiness. In 1954, Dr. Julian Rotter identified two types of people. The first type had an internal locus of control. They believed that ultimate control over the direction of their lives lay within themselves. Their choices, effort, and thoughts determined where they would end up. The second type of people believed that they had an external locus of control. Their lives were controlled fully by their family members, employers, genetics, or friends. They did not believe that their actions or choices truly mattered.

Rotter put these two types of people on opposite ends of a spectrum, and contended that everyone would fall somewhere along this line. Sixty years have passed, and numerous research studies on the topic have shown that compared to those who believe in an external locus of control, people who fall closer to the internal locus of control end of this spectrum are more likely to be satisfied at and perform well at work, school and home. They are healthier and happier than those who feel less in control of their lives.

"Science seems to have settled the question. People are free to determine their lives. What's the point of talking about this in English class?" You say to me. Be careful, dear reader, for things are a little more complicated than they seem. Having an internal locus of control can be dangerous when one is faced with powerful circumstances. For example, believing that you can convince your parents not to separate if they have already decided on this course of action might only set you up for disappointment. The way I understand it, having an internal locus of control does not mean that you think you are more powerful than any other person, or force. It just means that you understand your capacity for influencing your circumstances, even if you don't hold all the power.

I have come to understand that my level of agency (the extent to which I can control my life) does not remain constant over time. Instead, there are peaks and valleys. There are times in my life when I have very little control, and there are times when I am able to make decisions that will significantly change my path. In fact, the times in my life where I have very little control are often the result of significant choices I have made. Choosing what school to attend and choosing what activities to sign up for at the beginning of the year are examples of periods of agency. In these times, effort put into shaping your life will be more successful than effort you try to expend once you have committed to a course of action. If you are in a period of agency, treat it carefully. Try to make choices that will be aligned not just with what you want now, but what you might want a few years from now. If you are not in a period of agency, adjust your expectations accordingly. Either look for small ways to improve your current experience, or try to determine when your next period of agency will be coming around.

Regardless of your overall level of agency, there will always be opportunities for you to exert control over your life. One opportunity that will always exist is the opportunity to decide how to think about your life and circumstances. You will always be able to reframe a situation in a way that will help you learn from it, or escape it. For example, a menial job such as data entry can give you a chance to practice mindfulness.

The older I get, the more I realize that human beings are expert rationalizers. We can convince ourselves of almost anything, so long as it aligns with some of our pre-existing beliefs. This ability may seem frighteningly open to abuse, but I understand why people are like this. The older I get, the more I also realize that absolute truth is a prize that moves further away the more one runs to it. There is so much to know, and so many angles from which to know it. When I am determining whether to adopt a belief, I tend to look at the implications of the belief. Will these thoughts be useful for me and others? When we ask this question of internal locus of control, the answer is yes. This belief reveals more of the world to us. Having an internal locus of control is important because it will reveal these opportunities to you. If you believe that you have at least some power to change your circumstances, you will look for opportunities to have influence, and, if they exist, you will find and use them. If you believe that your life is totally determined by forces much stronger than yourself, you will not even bother to look for any opportunities to assert your vision.

Sources

Cherry, K. (2014). 'What is locus of control?' *Personality Psychology*. About Education. www.psychology.about.com/od/personalitydevelopment/fl/What-Is-Locus-of-Control.htm

Salmanhson, K. (2011). 'The no. 1 contributor to happiness.' *Psychology Today*. www.psychologytoday.com/blog/bouncing-back/201106/the-no-1-contributor-happiness

KEEP
SCANNING

KEEP SCANNING: RANDOMNESS

In his fantastic book *The Drunkard's Walk: How Randomness Rules our Lives*, physicist Leonard Mlodinow shares some surprising information. The first book of the Harry Potter series was rejected 12 times. It was read by 12 different publishers who decided that it would not sell. In this case, of course, 13 proved to be a lucky number, as the Harry Potter series became a global phenomenon. What separated J K Rowling from thousands of other rejected writers? She kept submitting her manuscript. Of course, a publishing deal is no guarantee of success, but the probability is higher than zero, which is more than we can say for a person who stops trying. What was it about the 13th submission that made it different? The reviewer had a young daughter who read the manuscript, and it was her interest that changed his mind.

We live in a complex world. Many moving parts have to align for something incredible to happen to us, whether that is meteoric success in the literary world, or starting a successful business. Many of these moving parts are things we can't control. How could J K Rowling have guessed that the 13th reviewer liked to share manuscripts with his daughter? How could you know that a contest you just entered actually had very few entrants? The three parts of the equation you can control are talent, effort and exposure. You can enhance your talent through careful study and practice, you can keep up your effort (perhaps by adopting a growth mindset as discussed in our Grit section), but I think that the third domain, exposure, is an underappreciated asset.

Exposure means giving yourself as many opportunities to be successful as makes sense. If you are a photography buff, it means entering as many competitions as you can manage. If you are interested in finding a girlfriend, you have a better chance of success if you try to meet new people than if you stay in your room.

You can increase your exposure if you keep scanning for opportunities. Scanning is a great habit to build, and is not that hard to start. If you set up your web browser so that a few pages that are relevant to your interests automatically load, information will come to you. Signing up for email newsletters has a similar effect. Even the groups you join on Facebook can bring new items to your attention. A little bit of Googling can also get you loads of information. Chances are, regardless of your area of interest, there are people who are sharing information and tips about it. Join that conversation and reap the benefits.

Nicholas Nassim Taleb, a successful trader on Wall Street and philosophy buff, makes the distinction between 'extremistan' and 'mediocristan' in his book *Antifragile*. Pursuits that lie within extremistan include writing, making music, and creating companies. What defines them is their 'winner take all' nature. There are millions of books with very few sales, but only a select few books with millions of sales. The winners take all. The potential upside is enormous (and non-linear), but it is not guaranteed. In mediocristan, however, rewards are pretty much guaranteed, and tied linearly to effort. Working in a retail clothing store is an example. Even if your pay is tied to commission, your effort in the store is tied pretty linearly to your reward, and you are guaranteed at least some pay even if things don't go so well. Compare this to an aspiring novelist. She has no guarantees of income, but there is a tiny chance that, like J K Rowling, she will grow to become a billionaire.

In your life, there are probably domains that use the rules of extremistan, and ones that use the rules of mediocristan. Overall, school is an example of mediocristan. Your effort results in a knowable payoff (grades, advancement to further education) that is (mostly) linearly tied to effort and talent. Still, individual aspects of your schooling can be shunted over to extremistan territory if they are 'stacked' with other purposes. For example, an open-ended art project can become a novella that you submit to a major contest (which, if you win, could open up more opportunities to write).

It is helpful to have a mixture of activities in your life, some that use the rules of mediocristan, and some that behave like extremistan. When you are engaged in extremistan activities and things aren't going well, I would encourage you to remember that failing repeatedly does not make you a failure. The moving parts of the world just may not have aligned themselves to allow for your success at this moment. Who knows what will happen tomorrow, or in five years? Improving your skills, maintaining a sustainable amount of effort, and increasing your exposure are your recipe for success, but only if you are patient. You have to find a way to enjoy the process in the absence of results. That is perhaps the biggest challenge of all, especially for a generation like ours that has been raised on instant-gratification electronic media!

Sources

Wilborn, A. (2013). 'Five hilarious reasons publishers rejected classic best-sellers'. *Cracked*. www.cracked.com/article_20285_5-hilarious-reasons-publishers-rejected-classic-best-sellers.html

Mlodinow, L. (2009). 'The drunkard's walk: how randomness rules our lives'. *Vintage Books*: London.

Taleb, N. (2012). 'Antifragile: things that gain from disorder'. *Random House*: New York.

SURF
THE
SNOWBALLS

SURFING AND SNOWBALLS

One of the taglines of a Canadian science video series I used to watch in grade school was "Inertia is a property of matter." You probably know what that means, but just to refresh your memory, things at rest tend to stay at rest, and moving things tend to stay moving. Of course, this doesn't take friction into account! Still, I am surprised by how well this physical law plays out metaphorically in life. Once you overcome the inertia of your life, and get it moving, it tends to stay in motion. Things snowball, and you get many more rewards than you might have expected for the effort you put in.

Actors and writers who talk about their 'big break' are people who understand the non-linear nature of the world very well. My own experience has come more in the domain of scholarships and awards. The more you win, the more you tend to win, both because you tend to be better at applying for them and because your recent awards make you a great candidate.

Inertia is not always a force for progress. Remember, it is also the force that keeps still things still. Inertia is why many people who are born poor stay poor (they do not have the resources and effort required to overcome this inertia), and why the rich keep getting richer (success leads to success leads to success). Much like a physical law, inertia is a fact of life. It may compound inequalities, but spending your time resenting this fact won't change its power. All you can do is understand and use this force for your own goals (which might even involve empowering the poor).

Overcoming inertia is the first and most difficult step to accomplishing something meaningful. Understanding that, after a certain point, your efforts might start to give you oversized returns will give you the hope you need to persevere. Developing momentum doesn't necessarily mean that things will be easy. What it does mean is that you will stop having to fight with yourself to convince yourself to practice your guitar each day, or to email a few different writers every Friday. So long as you are engaging in them mindfully, activities do get easier as you get more practice.

Still, working hard at a project (or an application, or a contest entry) is no guarantee of success. When we consider external momentum, that is, how the world responds to your efforts, we are again faced with the fact that life is non-linear. We talked about the useful side of this spectrum, where little effort can lead to big rewards, but it follows that there is another end of this spectrum, where herculean efforts don't lead to anything. To succeed in a world like ours, it is necessary to keep trying for that 'big break,' and to ensure that even our losses result in some gain. Building skill in an area is something that can never be taken away from you, regardless of the outcome, especially if you use whatever feedback you get to improve yourself.

Building internal momentum while hoping for external momentum is the best advice I can give you for learning how to live with the non-linearity of the world around you. I like to use the metaphor of surfing to help me understand the dynamics of my life. There will always be forces so powerful that they could throw me around like a ragdoll, but if I find a way to align my own energy with the direction of the force, I can tap into its power rather than being controlled. Starting to paddle from a standstill is quite an undertaking, but once I start to move, it becomes easier. Still, this internal momentum is nothing compared to the waves around me. I need to align myself with these large waves if I ever hope to ride into the beach.

A useful implication of this metaphor is that you are not done once you surf a wave. The point of tapping into external momentum is not so that you never expend effort again. It is so that you are ready to engage with the next challenge that comes your way. Much more of your time will be spent preparing to achieve something that you will spend achieving and enjoying it (the 'it' is a target that will always change). Using the metaphor of surfing might help you understand how to enjoy the process of fighting and channeling the forces that are around you.

LOVE YOUR
FUTURE SELF

LOVING FUTURE SELF

If you were a giraffe, life would be much simpler. You would be aware of what was around you, but only that. If a predator came, you would react. If you smelled a lady giraffe, you might walk over and investigate. If you were hungry, you would find something to eat. You would not think about mathematics or the opera, and you would not really have a conscious understanding of yourself. According to the Hauser Lab at Harvard University, one of the four main cognitive features that separates us from other animals like the giraffe is our ability to think about things that are outside of our present experience. This ability is called abstraction. Your first association with that word might be the difficult to decipher blobs of paint on a modernist canvas, but thinking about your grandmother when you are on your way to meet her is an example of abstraction. Considering your options for breakfast counts as abstraction too. In both cases, the object of your thought did not come from your environment; it was conjured by your mind (The 'real' object might exist somewhere else in space and time, but it is the distance between you and it that matters).

As they say, "If you are a human, don't act like a giraffe." Okay, perhaps no one ever said that, but there is one application of abstract thinking that I think you will find especially helpful. I call it "future self." Have you ever thought about yourself in the future? Who you will be, what you will dream about, where you will live, and even what you will eat? Sometimes, when you are faced with a choice that will benefit you in the present, but be bad for you in the future, it is useful to think about your future self. Human beings have a bias towards the tangible. We tend to value future benefits much less than what we can get right now. Simply put, $10 in two years or $5 now is an easy choice for most of us. And while this makes sense, broadly, because there is a chance that we will have no future in which to enjoy these long-term gains (because we might get eaten by lions), in the more probable scenario that we will live to see a few more decades, these short-sighted choices will cause us no end of trouble. It might feel good to put off studying for our math exam so we can play SpaceLord the video game, but when we fail the exam and need to take summer school, we'll realize that it wasn't worth it.

One of the issues with thinking about the future is that we (obviously) cannot manufacture a vivid picture of it. People can't say with certainty where they will be in ten years, or whether their hard work will pay off. Still, we do know that keeping up with a healthy diet and getting regular exercise will reduce our risks of illnesses. We do know that completing our education will give us a better chance of career satisfaction and success. We do know that the earlier we find the niche for our talents and begin honing them, the better our prospects will be. And yet, it can be so tempting to skip the gym, eat potato chips, postpone thinking about our futures, and neglect our school work. In short, we find it easier to be mean to our future selves than to say no to our present selves.

One way of attacking this problem is to use the habit-building sections of this book, but sometimes we need emotional motivation. I suggest having a picture of your future self. It can be a physical print (there are many free websites that will let you age your picture), or it can just be a vision in your head. Put a face on your future – your own face, that is. Try to call this image to your mind when you can feel your present and future selves in conflict. Try to love the person you will become as much as you love the person you are now.

I keep my future self in the back of my mind, but recently I realized that I was not 'closing the loop.' My present self was sacrificing its satisfaction, but never receiving any credit. I had forgotten about my past self! Now, when I make a good choice and reap the benefits in the future (even when it is as simple as meeting a fitness goal), I think about past Brianna with love and gratefulness. In both cases, I am using abstract thinking to try to bridge the gap between who I am, who I was and who I want to be. I am using the mental gifts that separate me from giraffes, and you can too!

Sources

Wolchover, N. (2011). 'What distinguishes humans from other animals?'. *LiveScience*. www.livescience.com/33376-humans-other-animals-distinguishing-mental-abilities.html

www.in20years.com

CPSIA information can be obtained
at www.ICGtesting.com
Printed in the USA
LVHW05s0058260718
584896LV00014B/703/P

9 781909 717756